Willing to Wait

Jan Black, Author

Steve Hunt and Dave Adamson, Design and Illustration

*We, the people who made this book,
like to help kids be willing to wait.*

*And the One who helped all of us was God,
Who wants even more than we do to help you
be willing to wait.*

A Publication of

ASSOCIATION OF CHRISTIAN SCHOOLS INTERNATIONAL

P.O. Box 35097 Colorado Springs, Colorado 80935-3509

Scripture taken from THE HOLY BIBLE, NEW INTERNATIONAL VERSION. Copyright © 1973, 1978, 1984 by the International Bible Society. Used by permission of Zondervan Bible Publishers.
NOTE: In order to make all references to God clear to students, we have chosen to capitalize pronouns referring to deity rather than follow the uncapitalized form of the NIV.

Willing to Wait
TABLE OF CONTENTS

things to know about this book...

Welcome to
WILLING TO WAIT!

Why was this book written?

Books are written for many reasons. This book was written to help you think about life. It will show you choices you can make at your age that will help you aim your life in God's direction.

Aiming your life in God's direction is smart, because God is the Maker of life. He is the expert and He knows what makes life count. The best part of God's way of life is that it has a happy ending: Heaven. And Heaven will be worth the WAIT!

What is inside this book?

WAITING for you on the pages of this book are words and pictures that are divided into units.

At the beginning of each unit is a story about a great hero and leader named Nehemiah. The pages about Nehemiah are marked with this 👤 . When you see 👤 in the Table of Contents, you will know where to find the Nehemiah stories.

At the end of each unit is THE WAITING ROOM. There you will learn how to wait for things like pets, Christmas, and sports seasons. When you see [The Waiting Room] in the Table of Contents, you will know THE WAITING ROOM is on that page.

Each unit is divided into three PARTS. Turn back one page to the Table of Contents. What are the parts called?
PART _____, PART _____, and PART _____.

Inside each PART are things to read, do, and talk about.

There are TWISTERS **TWISTER** to twist your tongue and give you important messages.

There are WAITING WORDS [🎤] that tell you what real kids your age think about waiting.

There are | Being free of lies. | **Honesty** | Being full of lies | at the bottom of many pages to remind you of what you are learning and what it means.

And there are other things in the book. But you'll have to WAIT to see them because they wouldn't all fit on this page.

What do I do now?

You turn to page 90 and fill in the section called MY EARLY IDEAS ABOUT WAITING.

NEHEMIAH

A story of a good idea

In this book you will learn about a man who had a good idea from God. He found out that the town God had given to his people was in a sad mess. The walls of the city were broken down, and the gates were burned. Those who lived there were miserable, and people from other towns were making fun of them and of their God.

This is a story of a brave and caring man, of hard-working and loyal people, and of a loving and wise God. It is the story of Nehemiah (Nee-uh-my-uh).

The Town is Down

ªIn the month of Kislev, which is sort of December, in the citadel of Susa,
An old family friend returned from a trip to his former homeland, Judah.

ᵇNehemiah inquired of the old family friend, Hanani was his name,
"How are things in the land we love? How's life for those who remain?"

ᶜHanani's report, unpleasant to hear, caused Nehemiah to pace.
"Jerusalem's broken, its gates have been burned. Our people are in disgrace."

ᵈNehemiah wept and went without food, spending his days in prayer.
"O Lord, God of heaven, the awesome One, I pray for Your people there."

ᵉForgive us, O God, for turning from You. Please remember Your promise to Moses.
Help us rebuild Jerusalem's wall, and defeat the ones that oppose us."

ᶠNehemiah's mind would not release the dream of the rebuilt wall.
His heart hung on its vision; his ears heard the distant call.

---

1. Nehemiah heard about the shame of the city from _____. Kislev is a Jewish month that happened

   about the same time as our month of _____ .

2. What was Nehemiah's good idea? _____

3. What is a good idea you have had? _____

4. If you were hoping to rebuild a wall in another town, what is one thing you would do first? _____

   _____

5. What do you think of Nehemiah so far? _____

Happy Promises from God

The way to know God's ideas about life is to read them in the book He has written. That book is called the Bible. The Bible is like a training guide. It tells us what to do and how to do it. Best of all, the Bible tells us what God is like.

Learning parts of the Bible so well that you can carry them in your mind is a smart idea. Why? Because God's own words can give you hope and help anytime you need them.

One part of the Bible that will give you hope and help for the rest of your life is found in the book of Psalms. In Chapter 37, God says this:

> [4]*Delight yourself in the LORD*
> *and He will give you the desires of your heart.*
>
> [5]*Commit your way to the LORD; trust in Him and He will do this:*
> [6]*He will make your righteousness shine like the dawn,*
> *the justice of your cause like the noonday sun.*
>
> [7]*Be still before the LORD and wait patiently for Him;*
> *do not fret when men succeed in their ways,*
> *when they carry out their wicked schemes.*
>
> [23]*The LORD delights in the way of the man whose steps He has made firm;*
> [24]*though he stumble, he will not fall,*
> *for the LORD upholds him with His hand.*
>
> [27]*Turn from evil and do good;*
> *then you will always live securely.*
>
> [28]*For the LORD loves the just*
> *and will not forsake His faithful ones.*

There are many happy and hopeful promises from God in these verses. These promises are for those who choose to live life God's way.

Read them over again and choose three favorites. Write one in each of these Promise Boxes.

Sometimes Tim wonders why he gets into more trouble when he is around Aaron than when he is around Jason. Sometimes Susan doesn't like obeying her big sister. And sometimes Jessica likes hearing about what is right more than she likes doing it. You, too? Then this unit could be a big help to you!

Fill in the facts as you find them.

Wisdom

Wisdom means: _____

_____

God's thoughts about wisdom: _____

_____

Nehemiah showed wisdom by: _____

_____

One way that I have been wise: _____

_____

Obedience

Obedience means: _____

_____

God's thoughts about obedience: _____

_____

Nehemiah showed obedience by: _____

_____

One way that I have been obedient: _____

_____

Responsibility

Responsibility means: _____

_____

God's thoughts about responsibility: _____

_____

Nehemiah showed responsibility by: _____

_____

One way that I have been responsible: _____

_____

Nehemiah asks permission to leave his job as cupbearer long enough to rebuild the wall.

NEHEMIAH

The Dream is Tested

*a*Nehemiah wisely kept his dream a secret from the rest
Until he felt the time was right to put it to a test.

*b*The time was four months later, in the month they called Nisan.
The test was telling his boss, the King, what it was he wanted
done.

*c*Nehemiah was looking sad that day, though he never had
before.
The King said, "Why the sadness? What makes your heart so
sore?"

*d*With fear and respect he told the king that Jerusalem's walls
had crumbled.
"The land of my fathers lies in disgrace. You are right to sense I
am troubled."

*e*The King asked Nehemiah if there was anything he could do.
Nehemiah spoke a silent prayer, then said, "Yes, if it pleases you."

*f*The King was pleased to listen and to fill his servant's needs.
So Nehemiah, man with a dream, had permission to proceed.

1. Find and circle the word "wisely." "Wisely" means "acting with wisdom." Why was it wise for Nehemiah to keep

   his idea a secret for awhile? _____

   _____

2. Can you think of a time it would have been wise for you to keep an idea to yourself for awhile?

   _____

   Now think of a time that you did behave wisely. Write it on the Information Page under "One way that I have
   been wise."

3. King Artaxerxes was not used to Nehemiah looking sad. What does that tell you about Nehemiah?

   _____

4. Do you get the feeling from the story so far that Nehemiah was an obedient servant? Yes _____ No _____
   Be ready to explain your reasons. Think about a time that you were obedient even though it was not easy.
   Write about it on the Information Page under "One way that I have been obedient."

5. Being a cupbearer could be a dangerous job. Why? What does having a job like this tell us about the kind

   of man Nehemiah was? _____

   _____

6. Doing his job for four months without complaining about his sadness shows us that Nehemiah was a responsible servant. Think about a time that you were a responsible "servant" to your parents or teacher. Write about
   it on the Information Page under "One way that I have been responsible."

7. Would you like to have Nehemiah as a servant if you were king? Yes _____ No _____

Part A. WISDOM

A simple saying for you to say without your tongue twisting terribly.

WE WELCOME WISDOM WHILE WAVING WILDLY.

—————————————— TIM ——————————————

Tim is a boy who is known for doing right most of the time. He is easy to be around, he likes to have fun, and his friends and family can almost always depend on him for help.

Since the time that Tim was a little guy, he has heard grown-ups say, "Tim is such a good boy!" That's what Jason's mother said about him after school one day at the very moment Aaron and his friends walked by. It made Tim wish he were out of town.

Aaron and his friends are known for doing wrong and for hurting the feelings of others. Sometimes they do and say funny things, and they have even been known to be nice, but mostly they like to pick on people. Tim was their next target.

"Hey, Timmy-Timmy! Good little boy! Come over here and show us how nice you are," they said in their own smirky way. "C'mon, widdle boy, such a good widdle boy," said Aaron in baby-talk. Hearing Aaron talk that way made the kids that were standing nearby giggle. Inside themselves they were thinking how awful it would be to have Aaron do this to them. Tim hurried to the bus and sat in the back by himself.

On the bus, Tim was wondering if he should be more like Aaron so that he wouldn't get picked on again. In his mind, he decided to spend the next afternoon with Aaron and his friends to show them that he was more than just a "good little boy." He knew that most days they rode their bikes to the corner for an ice cream cone and then went to the park near the school. He would have to tell his best friend Jason that he couldn't practice soccer with him tomorrow. "But I won't tell him why," he said to himself.

I. Story Search
Check

- Place a "T" over the sentence that tells you the kind of person Tim is. _____
- Place an "A" over the sentence that tells you the kind of people Aaron and his friends are. _____
- Underline the events that you think made Tim feel sad and shaky. _____
- Draw a line around the section that tells you what Tim was thinking. _____
- Place a star in front of the words that tell you Tim's plans. _____

2. Read God's words about friends, and then finish the story of Tim the way you think it ended.

God's Words About Being Wise
"He who walks with the wise grows wise,
but a companion of fools suffers harm." Proverbs 13:20

This means that the wisdom and the foolishness of the people we spend time with rub off on us. It also means that a person with foolish friends will end up getting hurt.

Using what I know of God to make sound decisions.	Wisdom	Leaving God out of my decisions.

Tim's Afternoon with Aaron

by _____

_____

_____

_____

_____

_____

_____

_____

_____

_____

_____

_____

_____

_____

_____

_____

_____

3. Everyone who wisely does right over and over again has been hurt by fools who don't like wisdom.

Jesus was killed by men who hated wisdom and right. Nehemiah, too, suffered for doing right.

NAME ONE OTHER BIBLE PERSON WHO SUFFERED FOR DOING RIGHT:_____

NAME ONE PERSON IN YOUR LIFE WHO HAS DONE RIGHT EVEN WHEN OTHERS SAID OR DID MEAN THINGS:

_____

4. You have just written the names of two wise people. Think of what our world would be like if the wise stopped doing right because the foolish made fun of them. Would you want to live here?

5. What about you? When is it hard for you to be wise by doing right? What people make it easiest for you to be wise? What can you do NOW to help yourself become an adult who is wise?

6. If Tim asked you for advice, what would you tell him?

_____

_____

7. If you asked Jesus for advice about your problem with being wise, what do you think He would tell you?

_____

_____

Important notice!!! Stop and read this!!!

If you have trusted God to forgive your sins, then you can ask His help in living wisely. Plus, He will reward you in heaven for choosing wisdom.

You are wise if ... You do right. You choose to be with _____ friends. You trust God to help you be wise.	**You are foolish if ...** You do _____. You choose to be with foolish friends. You try to be wise without _____ _____.

8. Make a list in your mind called Actions of a Wise Friend. On it, list the ways you think a wise friend treats others.

WORDS ABOUT WAITING

from Aaron, age 9:
"It was hard for me to wait for soccer to start. It was hard waiting, but I made it."

Part B. OBEDIENCE

1. Inside of every person there is something that kicks and screams and pouts when forced to do what it is told.

> The kicking may not kick holes in the wall.
> The screaming may not alarm the neighbors.
> The pouting may not make the mouth frown.
> But it is there, inside every person, wanting to disobey.

Why?

Because inside every person who has ever lived – except Jesus – there is a self who likes to disobey. It is <u>natural</u> to disobey because our <u>nature</u> inside us has been messed up by sin. Sin will always lead us back to its home called rebellion.

2. Look up the word "rebellion" in your dictionary and write its meaning here:

_____

_____

There is a nature of rebellion in each of us that wants to say "No!" when told what to do.

3. That is why Susan grumbles when Janna, her big sister, tells her to _____.
4. That is why Jordan gripes when the manager at the bowling alley tells him to stop

_____

Doing what I am told to do.	Obedience	Doing what I am told not to do.

5. And that is why you groan inside when your teacher tells you to_____

_____

But God says:
"Obey your leaders and submit to their authority," Hebrews 13:17
This means that God expects us to
do what those in charge of us tell us to do.

6. It is kind of God to tell us what He expects of us. God is God and He makes the rules.

If we choose to obey His rules, then we will receive His rewards.
If we choose to disobey His rules, then we will receive His penalties.
It is up to us.

But ...

The great thing about God is that He wants us to receive His rewards for doing right, and He is willing to help us obey.

So ...

He gives us a new nature, His nature, that is able to do right. It is <u>natural</u> for the <u>new nature</u> to obey. When we trust God to forgive our sin because Jesus died for our sin, we are given a new nature.

Then ...

We have a choice.

7. If Susan is a child of God, she can choose which nature to follow: her old one or her new one. Her old one would tell her to _____ her sister. Her new one would tell her to _____ her sister.

8. If Jordan is a child of God, he can choose which nature to follow. His old one would tell him to _____ at the bowling alley. His new one would tell him to _____ at the bowling alley.

9. If you are a child of God, you can choose which nature to follow. Your old one would tell you to _____ . Your new one would tell you to _____ .

The new nature gives us the power to obey. God is kind to give us His nature to help us receive the rewards of obeying.

What to expect

10. What kinds of words and actions can you expect from others if you choose to obey?

_____

_____

_____

What kinds of words and actions can you expect from others if you choose to disobey?

_____

_____

_____

── Good News!!! ──
When we go to heaven we get to leave our old natures behind!

A simple saying for you to say without your tongue twisting terribly.

DALLYING DEFINITELY DOESN'T DAZZLE.

But wait!

"Is there ever a time when it is right not to obey?"
"Yes. When someone tells you to do something you know is wrong."

11. Make a list of some things people may tell you to do that are wrong.

_____

_____

_____

12. What do you think Nehemiah would tell your class about obeying?

_____

_____

Just think! If you are a child of God, you will be a friend of Nehemiah in heaven!

WORDS ABOUT WAITING

from Josh, age 9:
"I had to wait to go to our cabin. I kept hoping Dad would say, 'Let's just go early.' But he never did. Once we left, it was fun."

Josh's advice for waiting to go somewhere: "Just forget about it until you leave."

Part C. RESPONSIBILITY

Jessica enjoyed hearing Grandma tell her stories about the hard chores she used to do as a young girl. But when it came to doing chores herself, Jessica lacked responsibility.

Complete these pages about responsibility and then be ready with ideas to help a person like Jessica.

Wisdom from God for you about responsibility:
"Do not merely listen to the word, and so deceive yourselves.
Do what it says." James 1:22

1. What do you think God means by these words?_____

_____

2. What do you think some of Nehemiah's duties, or responsibilities, were?

_____

3. Do you think he did his duties well? Yes____ No____ What makes you think so?

_____

4. What are some of your duties, or responsibilities?

_____

5. How do you do your duties? Very Well____ Mostly Well____ So-so____ Poorly____

Doing what I know is my duty to do.   **Responsibility**   Ignoring my duty.

6. What duty do you enjoy the least? _____

What duty do you enjoy the most? _____

The Duty Jesus Chose

All of us have _____1_____: The duty of _____2_____ , the duty of _____3_____ , the duty of

_____4_____ of those we _____5_____ . Jesus chose the _____

_____6_____ . In Heaven, God the _____7_____ ,

God the _____8_____ , and God the _____9_____ chose duties.

God the Son accepted the duty of dying for the _____10_____ of the people on _____11_____.

At just the right time, He left _____12_____ and took on the form of a _____13_____ in its mother's

_____14_____ . The mother's name was _____15_____ . God sent an _____16_____ to tell her what was

happening. She was full of _____17_____ to think that God would let her body _____18_____ the

_____19_____ . It was a special _____20_____ .

Mary had the _____21_____ and He grew to be a _____22_____ and then a _____23_____

who was a _____24_____ of people. Many people were _____25_____

that God had come to earth. Others were _____26_____ when He told them who He was.

They _____27_____ the way God had planned things, after all. Even though Jesus

brought _____28_____ to those around Him, the angry people _____29_____

Him. It was a _____30_____ He knew He would have to do in order for the rest of us to be able to

go to _____31_____ . Because Jesus is God and _____32_____ ,

Jesus_____33_____ . Yet His duty was _____34_____ in place of us for

the wrong that we do. Sin's duty is to lead sinners _____35_____ . Jesus' duty was to lead sinners

_____36_____ . Our duty is to _____37_____ to let either sin or Jesus lead us. Jesus chose the

_____38_____ so that we could have the _____39_____ of living in Heaven

_____40_____ with Him.

40	forever	27	didn't like	13	baby	34	to die	38	duty of dying
2	cleaning	5	love	28	kindness and healing	15	Mary	32	God is perfect
14	womb	36	to God	16	angel	10	sin	17	joy
25	happy	30	duty	23	man	11	earth	19	Son of God
18	carry	9	Holy Spirit	3	helping	8	Son	29	killed
6	duty of dying	35	away from God	39	gift	31	Heaven	26	angry
4	taking care	7	Father	37	choose	1	duties	24	loving leader
21	baby	22	fine boy	12	Heaven	33	never once did wrong	20	responsibility

7. What ideas do you have to help a person with Jessica's problem?

_____

A YOUR TURN

A simple saying for you to say without your tongue twisting terribly.

_____

The Waiting Room

A waiting question: How long did Nehemiah wait to tell the King about his dream of rebuilding the wall?

_____

Waiting For a Pet

Brian, age 9, couldn't wait to get a cat. Here's what he says about it:

"I could not wait to get a new cat. I asked Mom over and over, 'When are we going to get a cat?' Soon after that I got mad. I went to my room and slammed the door, and there on my bed was a cat!"

Brian's Mom had planned quite a surprise. If Brian could have waited just a little longer before getting mad, how might his story have been different?

_____

_____

Pet Wisdom

What words of wisdom do you have for kids wanting pets? How should they choose their pet? What can they do to get ready for it?

_____

_____

_____

Be ready to talk about:

1. The reason many parents are nervous about letting their kids have pets.
2. The parts of owning a pet that take obedience and responsibility.
3. The ways you can prove you are able to care for a pet.
4. The pet you would most like to have.

Just think of it! Pets were God's idea to bring Him, and them, and us joy!

"Thank you, God, for pets!"

Be willing to wait for the right pet.

Are you ever told that you can't do something because you are too young? Everyone has grown up hearing that. But there are some things you <u>can</u> do now. This unit will tell you about a few of them. So, pay attention, have faith, and be sensitive to those things you can know and do at <u>any</u> age.

Fill in the facts as you find them.

Attentiveness

Attentiveness means: _____

_____

God's thoughts about attentiveness: _____

_____

Nehemiah showed attentiveness by: _____

_____

One way that I have been attentive: _____

_____

Faith

Faith means: _____

_____

God's thoughts about faith: _____

_____

Nehemiah showed faith by: _____

_____

One way that I have shown faith: _____

_____

Sensitivity

Sensitivity means: _____

_____

God's thoughts about sensitivity: _____

_____

Nehemiah showed sensitivity by: _____

_____

One way that I have been sensitive: _____

_____

Nehemiah takes a private tour of the wall at night.

NEHEMIAH

The Dream is Shared

^aWord travelled fast to Jerusalem through officials on the way. But two who heard became upset and said, "That'll be the day!"

^bSanballat and Tobiah, the two, were glad the wall was down. They liked shaming the Israelites and making fun of their town.

^cBut Nehemiah knew their kind. He knew they'd have a turn at being shamed for being glad Jerusalem had burned.

^dFor three long days he waited. Folks asked themselves, "What's cooking?"
Then one dark night he mounted up and silently went looking.

^eHe saw the crumbled, ruined wall, the sooty, charcoaled gates. And knew that God would help rebuild another in its place.

^fAnd, finally, he spoke the dream God placed inside his heart: "Let's build that wall again, my friends, and now's the time to start."

1. What were some of the things Nehemiah had to pay attention to as he arrived in Jerusalem?

   _____

   _____

   Write one of these on the Information Page under "One way Nehemiah showed attentiveness."

2. Pretend you are a young person in Nehemiah's time. You are standing near Sanballat and Tobiah, listening to them talk. What might you have heard them say? _____

   _____

   _____

   Now pretend you are standing near some people in town who don't know Nehemiah but have heard about him. What might they be saying? _____

   _____

   _____

3. How important do you think it was for Nehemiah to be a good listener?

   Very, very, very important _____ Very important _____ Sort of important _____
   In which part of the Nehemiah poem do you think Nehemiah did the most listening? Put a mark by it. Be ready to explain your answer.

4. Nehemiah spent three days in Jerusalem before taking a ride to look at the wall. Using your sensitivity, explain in a few words how he might have been feeling inside as he waited. _____

   _____

   _____

Part A. ATTENTIVENESS

A simple saying for you to say without your tongue twisting terribly.

Listeners learn lasting lessons.

Say the TWISTER five times in a row, then think of one lasting lesson you have learned by listening. Write it on the Information Page under "One way that I have been attentive."

── Is Anyone Listening ──

1. Two people are talking. Be a listener and decide what these two talkers are not doing.

"Hey, guess what! I got a letter from my brother over in Europe!"

"Do you still have my tire pump?"

"Man, I can hardly wait to wear it."

"I need it for the bike ride this afternoon."

"He says he bought me a jacket in Germany."

"I loaned it to someone. Probably Freddy."

"Well, see ya."

"Mom, have you seen my tire pump?"

2. What is missing in this talk?

These talkers have not been ＿ ＿ ＿ ＿ ＿ ＿ ＿ ＿ ＿.

       L   S   T   I   E   I   N   G   N

3. Change their talk by putting new words into their mouths.

Make their words show that they are ＿ ＿ ＿ ＿ ＿ ＿ ＿ ＿ ＿ ＿.

4. How was Nehemiah attentive?

Write your answer on the Information Page under "Nehemiah showed attentiveness by ..."

Watching and listening closely to what is happening.	**Attentiveness**	Neglecting to notice what is happening.

Listening Q's and A's

Are you a good LISTENER? Do you PAY ATTENTION to what others say?
Your teacher is going to read an important section from the Bible about the wisest man who ever lived. Listen, and then see what you remember by filling in the answers to these questions.

5. The wisest man was _____ .

6. His wisdom was given to him by _____ .

7. His understanding of things was as great as the _____ on the seashore.

8. He was famous in his own country and in other _____ .

9. He spoke _____ proverbs and wrote _____ songs.

10. He understood the secrets of _____ and taught about _____ and _____ ,
    _____ and _____ .

11. People from everywhere came to _____ to Solomon's wisdom.

    How fine a listener are you? Give yourself 20 points for every correct answer. Your score? _____ .

If Solomon were living now …

I WONDER IF PEOPLE WOULD ASK FOR HIS AUTOGRAPH.

I WONDER IF HE WOULD BE ON A TALK SHOW.

I WONDER IF HE WOULD FLY IN HIS OWN JET.

I WONDER IF _____

12. Solomon said something to his son that can be helpful to us. He said,

    "My son, pay attention to what I say; listen closely to my words. Do not let them out of your sight, keep them within your heart; for they are life to those who find them and health to a man's whole body."
    Proverbs 4:22

13. By PAYING ATTENTION to Solomon's words in the book of Proverbs in the Bible, you will be showing God that you care about your life. PLUS, you will be adding the wisdom of God to your life. Be smart. Be a LISTENER.

14. By PAYING ATTENTION to others you will be showing kindness, plus you will be able to understand what is going on. Be smart. Be a LISTENER.

15. Think about the people in your life. Which ones do you need to listen to the most?

    _____   _____

    _____   _____

    _____   _____

    It is smart and wise to be attentive. God will help you.

WORDS ABOUT WAITING

from Chris, age 9:
"I had to wait 4½ weeks for my skateboard, 8 days for my cat, and a long time for my friend to get back from Idaho."

Part B. FAITH

1. If God gave out report cards to groups of people, the early followers of God like Abraham and Job and Moses would get an "A." Why? Because they had faith in things they couldn't see with their eyes. Read about it for yourself:
"Now faith is being sure of what we hope for and certain of what we do not see. This is what the ancients were commended for."
Hebrews 11:1, 2

2. Put a line under the words "ancients" and "commended." Look them up in the dictionary, then write their meanings here:

Ancients _____

Commend _____

3. If God commends faith, then we would be wise to copy the ancients and show faith, too. Pleasing God is the most important thing we could ever do.

What is faith?

4. It is "being sure of _____."
What do Christians hope for? _____

_____

5. It is "being certain of _____."
What are Christians certain of but they don't see?

_____

_____

A simple saying for you to say without your tongue twisting terribly.

Faith-filled followers are fond of forever.

Believing God will do what He says He will do.	Faith	Disbelieving God.

You, the Private Eye

If you were a Private Eye looking for clues about God, you would find them everywhere. In fact, there would be too many for your file cabinet to hold. Fill out this report by naming some of the clues around us that show God is real.

CLUES IN THE ANIMAL WORLD

Think of the clues in the animal world. Were pigeons once eagles who decided to become pigeons? Do kangaroos have perfect pockets for their babies because they sewed them on?

Clues about God in the animal world: _____
_____
_____

CLUES IN THE UNIVERSE

Think of the clues in the universe. Did the planets just plop into place on their own? Is the moon hanging in the sky without help? Did the sun decide by itself to warm us just right?

Clues about God in the universe
_____
_____
_____

CLUES IN THE PEOPLE WORLD

Think of the clues in us! Do we have minds that can make spaceships because He made our minds?
_____
_____
_____

CLUES IN THE PLANT WORLD

Think of the clues in plants and trees. Do trees lose their leaves at the same time by chance? Did flowers have a meeting to decide who would look like what and when to bloom?

Clues about God in the plant world _____
_____
_____

OFFICIAL P.I. INVESTIGATION

OFFICIAL INVESTIGATION: FINAL CLUES ABOUT GOD

Clue #1 _____
_____

Clue #2 _____
_____

Clue #3 _____
_____

Clue #4 _____
_____

Clue #5 _____
_____

By faith I believe that God _____
_____
_____ .

Signed: _____ ,P.I.

How did Nehemiah show his faith in God so far in this story? Write your answer on the Information Page under "Nehemiah showed faith by:"

23

from Wendy, age 8:
"I think it's hard to wait to go on a picnic, to my friend's house and to go to Hawaii."

Part C. SENSITIVITY

Sensitivity is caring about the feelings and needs of others. This verse tells about a person who is NOT sensitive:

"Like one who takes away a garment on a cold day,
or like vinegar poured on soda,
is one who sings songs to a heavy heart."
Proverbs 25:20

1. How would your skin feel if your coat was taken away on a cold day? _____
If you were soda, how would you feel if vinegar was dropped on you? (Try it!)
That's how it feels when you are sad and others are so full of their own happiness that they miss your sadness.
God is sensitive to us. He cares about our feelings and our needs.

> **JUST THINK!** God cares about how you feel!
> Be glad that God is not selfish.

2. Jesus showed sensitivity to the people around Him.

How was He sensitive to the children? _____

_____

How was He sensitive to the blind man? _____

_____

How was He sensitive to Mary and Martha at the tomb of their brother? _____

_____

How was He sensitive to the thief next to Him on the cross? _____

_____

_____

Sensing the needs of others.   **Sensitivity**   Blocking out the needs of others.

3. You can show sensitivity to the people around you. How would you be sensitive to these people?

■ John's puppy was run over by a car yesterday. Last night you got a puppy for the first time.

■ Your father's boss gave him an extra stack of work to do tonight. Now Dad can't go with the family to your brother's ball game.

■ You didn't score well on your spelling test. The person next to you did.

■ Your mother just dropped and broke the plate her grandmother gave her for her wedding.

■ Your teacher planned to take you on a field trip today, but the bus broke down on the way to pick up your class. Now you can't go.

4. Sensitive Sentences.
Practice saying these sentences. Save them in your mind to use at the right time.

"I'm sorry you have to go through this."

"I'm happy for you."

"You did a good job!"

"I care about how you're feeling."

"I know you must be upset."

"I'm proud of you!"

Sometimes words don't do the job of caring. At those time, a gentle smile, a pat on the back, or a quiet visit say things words can't.

A YOUR TURN

A simple saying for you to say without your tongue twisting terribly.

_____

_____

The Waiting Room

Waiting for People

Waiting for people can be very boring. It can also be maddening, UNLESS we learn to wait for people the right way. Learning the right way to wait for people is smart because you will be doing it your whole life.

Jeanah, age 9, says:

"Once I had to wait for my Dad. We were at church and he was talking to people. I remembered about lunch. The time was 12:30. Finally Daddy stopped talking."

Randy, age 8, says:

"Yesterday my brother came to the car late. It was hard to wait for him."

Mark, age 8, says:

"Once my friend told me he would call. So I waited, waited, waited, and waited. And while I was waiting I did my homework. Then I went outside and picked tomatoes and corn from my garden. Then finally he called."

My Waiting Plan

As your class talks about ways to wait for people, write down some of the ideas you hear. Add any of your own.

HOW TO WAIT FOR A GROWN-UP TO STOP TALKING SO YOU CAN GO HOME:

_____

_____

_____

HOW TO WAIT FOR SOMEONE TO GET INTO THE CAR:

_____

_____

_____

HOW TO WAIT FOR A PHONE CALL:

_____

_____

_____

The energy a person uses getting mad over waiting for someone
just might be enough to help the late person be on time!

Welcome to Unit Three! On these pages you will get to use your clever mind to think up plans and ideas to happy-up your life and the lives of others. Plus, you will watch as Nehemiah faces his enemies with courage.

Fill in the facts as you find them.

Thankfulness

Thankfulness means: _____

_____

God's thoughts about thankfulness: _____

_____

Nehemiah showed thankfulness by: _____

_____

One way that I have been thankful: _____

_____

Orderliness

Orderliness means: _____

_____

God's thoughts about orderliness: _____

_____

Nehemiah showed orderliness by: _____

_____

One way that I have been orderly: _____

_____

Courage

Courage means: _____

_____

God's thoughts about courage: _____

_____

Nehemiah showed courage by: _____

_____

One way that I have been courageous: _____

_____

Sanballet and Tobiah mock as Nehemiah tells them that the God of Heaven will help the people rebuild the wall.

NEHEMIAH

The Work Begins

ªSanballat and Tobiah would ridicule and mock.
But Nehemiah let them know his faith was more than talk.

ᵇHe called the town together with work list in his hand,
And gave out gate assignments to every waiting man.

ᶜThe priests rebuilt the Sheep Gate and next to them were others.
The Fish Gate had its beams and doors built by a team of brothers.

ᵈThe Old Gate got its face lift from Meshullam and Joiada
The section next to it was fixed by Shallum and his daughters.

ᵉThe Valley Gate was rebuilt by a man named Hanun.
While Malkijah, on down the wall, rebuilt the gate called Dung.

ᶠThe remaining gates and walls were fixed by other courageous folks.

Nehemiah's orderly plan had worked, in spite of enemy jokes.

1. Read Section "a" again. How did Nehemiah show that his faith was more than talk?

_____

_____

2. Choose one sign of orderliness in this story and write it on the Information Page under, "One way Nehemiah was orderly."

3. For what do you think the workers were thankful? _____

4. Find Nehemiah 3:3 in your Bible. Read until the end of verse 5. On this line, write the names of two other people who worked near the Fish Gate. _____

_____

What group of people would NOT "put their shoulders to the work"? _____

_____

5. Why did rebuilding the wall take courage? _____

_____

When have you been ridiculed or mocked? _____

_____

6. What do you think has been Nehemiah's best show of courage? Write your answer on the Information Page.

Part A. THANKFULNESS

Are you a thanker?

1. What have you said "thank you" for so far today? _____

_____

Be glad if you have been trained to give thanks for things others do or say. (A good idea: Say "thanks" to your parents for teaching you to say "_____!") If you haven't been trained to give thanks, you can teach yourself! Thankers live happier days than non-thankers, because thanking is the *right* thing to do.

Saying "_____ _____" to people is kind and right.

Saying "_____ _____" to God is kind and right *and* brings Him glory.

It is amazing to think that with our own lips we can bring _____ to God by saying "_____

_____."

2.

What shall I thank Him for?

Here is a good place to start. You can find this verse in Psalm 136, verses 1, 2, 3, 4, and 26.

"Give thanks to the LORD, for He is good.
Give thanks to the God of gods.
Give thanks to the LORD of lords.
To Him who alone does great wonders.
Give thanks to the God of heaven.

His love endures forever.
His _____ endures forever.
His love _____ forever.
His love endures _____.
_____ l__v__ __nd__r__s f__r__v__r."

3. From these verses, for what 2 reasons can we say "_____ _____" to God?

1. _____

2. _____

4. What does "endure" mean? _____

How long will God's love for you last? _____

God's forever love is a forever reason to thank Him forever.

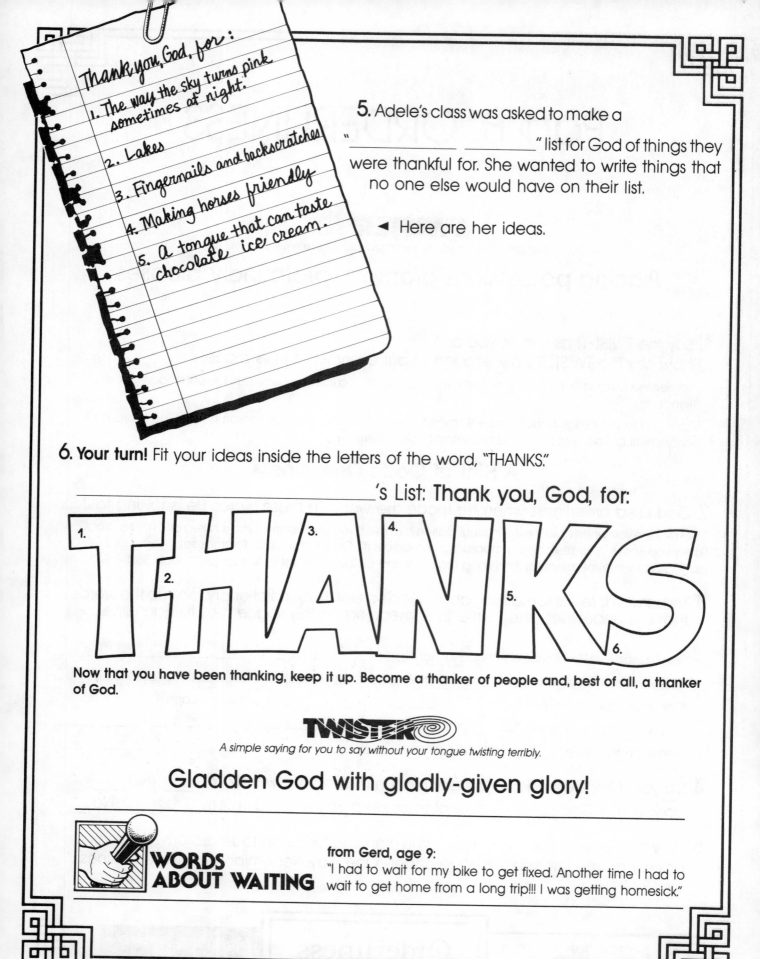

Thank you, God, for:
1. The way the sky turns pink sometimes at night.
2. Lakes
3. Fingernails and backscratches
4. Making horses friendly
5. A tongue that can taste chocolate ice cream.

5. Adele's class was asked to make a

"_____ _____" list for God of things they were thankful for. She wanted to write things that no one else would have on their list.

◄ Here are her ideas.

6. Your turn! Fit your ideas inside the letters of the word, "THANKS."

_____'s List: Thank you, God, for:

THANKS
1. 2. 3. 4. 5. 6.

Now that you have been thanking, keep it up. Become a thanker of people and, best of all, a thanker of God.

TWISTER

A simple saying for you to say without your tongue twisting terribly.

Gladden God with gladly-given glory!

WORDS ABOUT WAITING

from Gerd, age 9:
"I had to wait for my bike to get fixed. Another time I had to wait to get home from a long trip!!! I was getting homesick."

Part B. ORDERLINESS

A simple saying for you to say without your tongue twisting terribly.

Placing possessions promptly profoundly pleases.

1. Say the TWISTER as fast as you can.
Now, say the TWISTER slow enough to put every word in its place.

Sometimes our possessions get jumbled just like the words of a fast tongue twister. You can't figure out where things are.

Learning to put things in their place is smart for many reasons. The best reason is that God is orderly. If orderliness is God's way, then we are smart to be orderly, too.

A Hint of God's Orderliness

2. God used orderliness when he made the world. In these words He is talking to Job:

"Where were you when I laid the earth's foundation? Tell me, if you understand. Who marked off its dimensions? Surely you know! Who stretched a measuring line across it? On what were its footings set, or who laid its cornerstone while the morning stars sang together and all the angels shouted for joy?"   Job 38:4-7

3. These words tell us something about God's order. In your dictionary, look up the words that are underlined, then write their meaning on the space next to each line.

First, we read that He "laid the earth's <u>foundation</u>." _____

Next, we read that He "marked off its <u>dimensions</u>." _____

(Can you picture God stretching a _____ _____ across the earth?)

Next, we read that He set the "<u>footings</u>" of the earth. _____

Then we read that He laid the earth's "<u>cornerstone</u>." _____

4. Do you think God had an orderly plan in making the world? Yes ____ No ____
Do you think God has an orderly plan for keeping the world orderly? Yes ____ No ____

5. How did Nehemiah show orderliness in planning for his trip to Jerusalem? Write your answer on the Information Page under "One way Nehemiah showed orderliness."

Putting things and plans in their right place.	Orderliness	Allowing things and plans to become confusing.

Ned

6. These are sounds that Ned heard every day, except on December 24 when he cleaned his room for Christmas, and on the last day of school when he cleaned out his desk:

"Ned, Ned, your room is a mess. Where your bed is, I haven't a _____.
"Ned, Ned. Are you in _____? I'm certain you are, but I don't know where!"

"Ned, Ned, your desk is a _____. Finding a pen would take you all night!"
"Ned, Ned, where is your book? Dig in again for another _____."

Ned got used to hearing people moan about his messiness. But then his messiness began keeping him from doing things he enjoyed.

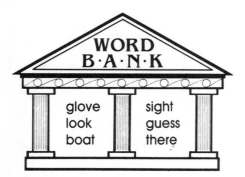

WORD
B·A·N·K

glove	sight
look	guess
boat	there

"Ned, Ned, get your coat, we're going to ride in the neighbor's
_____."
"I can't find my coat."

"Ned, Ned, grab your
_____. We're going to play and your team is up."
"I can't find my glove."

7. Ned decided he needed orderliness more than messiness. He asked Tim for help. If Ned had asked for your help, how would you have helped him put orderliness into his room and desk?

HOW TO PUT ORDERLINESS INTO A BEDROOM AND A DESK
by _____

Step 1. _____
Step 2. _____
Step 3. _____
Step 4. _____
Step 5. _____
Step 6. _____
Step 7. _____
Step 8. _____
Step 9. _____
Step 10. _____

8. After Ned became orderly, he heard new sounds. What were they?

"Ned, Ned, _____."

Make up your own rhyme.

WORDS ABOUT WAITING

from Sarah, age 9:
"One day I got dropped off at Anderson's after school and my mom was not there when I got there, so I was scared. But finally she came." WHAT COULD SARAH HAVE DONE IF MOM HADN'T SHOWN UP UNTIL MUCH LATER?

Part C. COURAGE

PRETEND that someone tells you to:
1. Do drugs or leave.
2. Steal a record from a store or be blamed for it anyway.
3. Keep quiet about seeing the big kid next door dent the car or you'll get dented.
4. Leave with them or your family will get hurt.

WHAT WOULD YOU SAY OR DO?

1. _____
2. _____
3. _____
4. _____

It takes courage to do right. Start building your own courage by listening to stories about other people's courage. At a time when some grown-ups are feeling relaxed, ask them to tell you some true stories of courage.

God promises to give courage to His children who choose to do right. When you choose to do right, the courage will come.

The three Hebrew boys in the story of Daniel received courage from God when they chose to do right, even when it meant losing their lives. They said:

"… O Nebuchadnezzar, we do not need to defend ourselves before you in this matter. If we are thrown into the _____ furnace, the God we serve is able to save us from it, and He will _____ us from your hand, O king. But _____ if He does not, we want you to know, O king, that we will _____ serve your gods or _____ the image of gold you have set up."
Daniel 3:16-18

WORD B·A·N·K

rescue	not
blazing	even
worship	

| Facing danger or ridicule without turning away. | Courage | Giving in to the fear of danger or ridicule. |

What other people in the Bible showed COURAGE? (Don't forget Nehemiah!)

THE PERSON   **HOW HE/SHE SHOWED COURAGE**

_____

_____

_____

_____

_____

_____

You can become known as a person of COURAGE, too. It is your choice.

A YOUR TURN

TWISTER

A simple saying for you to say without your tongue twisting terribly.

_____

_____

A VERY LARGE AND FRIENDLY WORD FIND

```
R  W  W  I  S  D  O  M  E  A  S  T  W  I  S  T  E  R  D  F
E  B  A  F  N  K  K  L  K  N  N  H  Z  X  B  K  V  D  O  I
S  E  I  L  B  C  G  J  M  O  O  A  N  Q  T  J  U  R  W  N
P  C  T  B  L  R  Q  O  M  K  I  N  H  B  J  N  D  U  I  G
O  T  I  D  E  L  S  O  B  V  D  K  S  R  Z  E  P  C  I  O
N  H  N  E  H  E  M  I  A  H  N  F  T  B  R  I  L  T  B  N
S  A  G  Y  T  G  M  N  D  W  R  U  Z  L  S  J  B  E  D  F
I  D  F  R  W  A  P  Q  T  U  Z  L  I  O  M  N  D  A  A  Q
B  F  G  I  J  R  L  M  W  S  E  N  S  I  T  I  V  I  T  Y
I  D  B  Z  Y  U  W  V  T  R  E  E  P  O  E  K  T  I  G  E
L  Q  S  O  L  O  M  O  N  S  R  S  T  N  V  H  W  Z  X  Y
I  P  O  N  M  C  L  K  S  J  I  S  C  G  F  E  D  C  B  A
T  M  C  U  P  B  E  A  R  E  R  E  L  E  Y  J  B  K  D  M
Y  R  Q  D  B  W  N  A  T  T  E  N  T  I  V  E  N  E  S  S
```

Hidden in these letters are words you have seen so far in this book. They are listed at the bottom of this page.

Cross off each word on the list as you find it.

One word is a bonus word, but you'll have to WAIT to find out if you found it! Happy circling!!

THE BONUS
WORD:

_____

Waiting	Sensitivity	Cupbearer
Attentiveness	Orderliness	Nehemiah
Solomon	Twister	Courage
Faith	Responsibiilty	Obedience
Wall	Wisdom	Thankfulness

The Waiting Room

Waiting for a Meal

Waiting for food happens every day, but Joshua, age 8, doesn't like it. He says:
"When my mom is making dinner and I get hungry, I don't feel like waiting, but I have to."

1. Why does Joshua have to wait? What does this tell you about Joshua? About his mother?

2. How does your stomach feel when you are very hungry? _____

_____

How does your stomach sound when you are very hungry? _____

_____

3. What can a person do to make waiting for food a little easier? _____

_____

Ideas for making food-waiting a little easier

_____

_____

_____

_____

_____

_____

_____

Be ready to talk about:

- Games your mind can play while sitting in a restaurant.
- Stories or jokes you can tell the others at the table.
- The food that makes you feel hungry when you smell it cooking.
- Your best meal ever.

Hello again! You're about to meet falling people, loyal people, joyful peole, and waiting people. The falling people are tripping over their pride; the loyal people are facing danger over their promises; the joyful people are celebrating about their God; and the waiting people are waiting for you-know-what.

Fill in the facts as you find them.

Meekness

Meekness means: _____

_____

God's thoughts about meekness: _____

_____

Nehemiah showed meekness by: _____

_____

One way that I have been meek: _____

_____

Loyalty

Loyalty means: _____

_____

God's thoughts about loyalty: _____

_____

Nehemiah showed loyalty by: _____

_____

One way that I have been loyal: _____

_____

Joy

Joy means: _____

_____

God's thoughts about joy: _____

_____

Nehemiah showed joy by: _____

_____

One way that I have been joyful: _____

_____

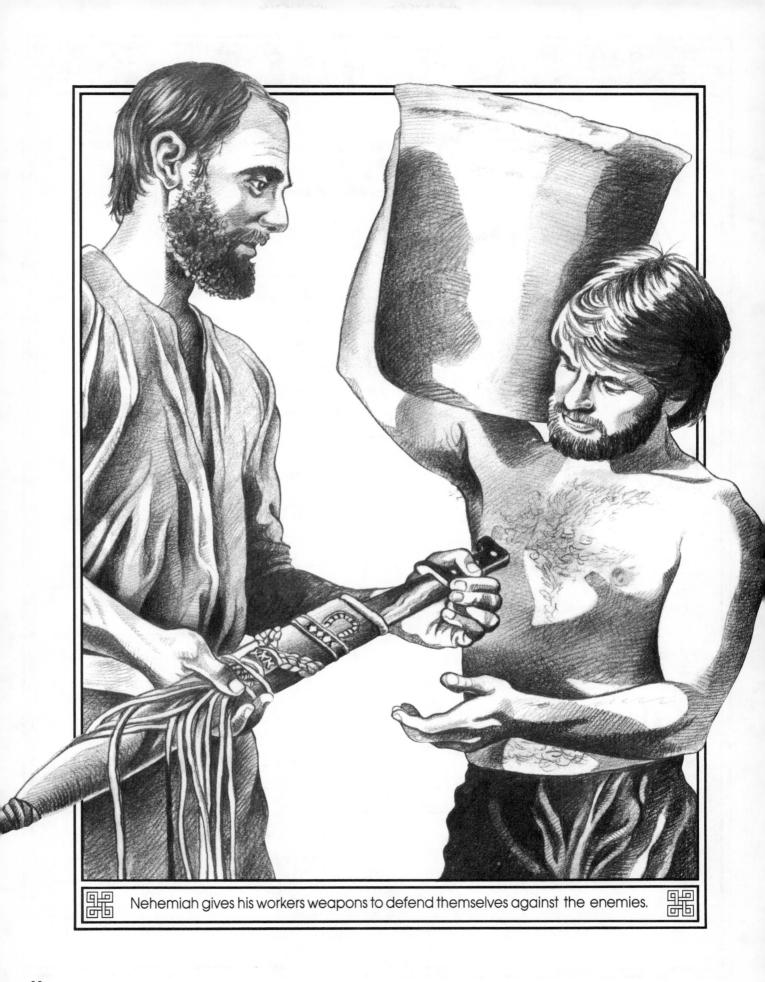

Nehemiah gives his workers weapons to defend themselves against the enemies.

NEHEMIAH

The Danger Grows

ᵃ Sanballat and Tobiah filled the air with jeers.
They mocked the builders of the wall with snickering and sneers.

ᵇ Sanballat called them "feeble Jews" in front of all his friends.
They laughed at every smirky slur Sanballat's mouth could send.

ᶜ Tobiah, full of wicked pride, said in taunting tones,
"If a fox climbed up there, he'd break their wall of stones!"

ᵈ When half the wall was finished, the mocking turned to threats.
"Let's kill those Jews and end their work," the enemies all said.

ᵉ The builders and the leaders went to God in prayer,
Then Nehemiah posted guards and told them to beware.

ᶠ The loyal crew kept working with tool and spear in hand.
They trusted God to help them build the wall around His land.

1. There are many events in Nehemiah's story that wouldn't fit into this unit's poem. Choose two of those events you think are most exciting. _____

2. Circle the word "loyal" in the poem. How did the crew show their loyalty?
_____

3. Would you say that Sanballat and Tobiah showed meekness or pride? _____

4. If Nehemiah were trusting God to fight for them, why did he give his workers weapons? _____
_____

5. Do you think the trumpet player enjoyed his job? Yes _____ No _____
Do you think he was glad he hadn't stopped taking lessons? Yes _____ No _____

6. On the Information Page, write one way Nehemiah showed meekness in this story.

7. This was a scary time for the workers and for Nehemiah. But even in scary times, we can have joy. What joy do you think Nehemiah had? Write your answer on the Information Page.

Part A. MEEKNESS

IF YOU THINK YOU ARE, YOU'RE NOT!

Thinking you are cool means one thing: You aren't cool. Kids and grown-ups who act like they are better than other people are proving that they are not. When we act smug and cool, we had better watch out because we are headed for trouble.

A simple saying for you to say without your tongue twisting terribly.

The smug surely swagger to a sorry stumble.

1. Here's what Wisdom says about pride (the kind of pride which makes you think you are better than others):

"Pride goes before destruction, a haughty spirit before a fall."
Proverbs 16:18

2. Look up these words in your dictionary:

Pride _____

Destruction _____

Haughty _____

Smug _____

3. If pride will cause us to break, or fall, what do you suppose meekness will do?

_____

From what you know of pride and meekness so far,
would you say it is smarter to learn to be meek or to be proud?
Meek _____ Proud _____

4. The pride that makes us think we are cool is different than the pride that helps us want to do our work well or keep our hair combed. Taking pride IN ourselves is right, but being proud OF ourselves OVER others is wrong.

Here is what PRIDE IN ourselves would say:	Here is what PRIDE OF ourselves would say:
"I want to do my best because doing my best is right."	"I want to do my best so that people will think I am great."
"I like the way I look with my hair like this."	"Having my hair like this makes me look better than anyone."
"I enjoy drawing. I want to learn to draw really well."	"Wait'll they see my picture. They'll hate theirs when they see mine."

| Serving others with the abilities God has given me. | **Meekness** | Showing off with the abilities God has given me. |

40

Watch out for falling people

5. What kinds of falling does pride cause? All kinds! Like these:

a. Celia saw the teacher's grade book. She saw that she had the highest grade so far on yesterday's math test. She wanted everyone to know about it, so during reading she whispered loudly to Brandon, "I got the highest score on the math test." Her mouth wore a smirk. Later that day, the teacher finished correcting the rest of the tests. She said, "Michael and Ramona tied for the highest score on the math test yesterday. They each got a 98."

b. Jim felt smug about being chosen to lead the flag salute in chapel. He knew that Danny had hoped to be chosen to do it. On his way to the platform, Jim turned to look at Danny to be sure he was watching. Jim didn't see Mrs. Brock standing there, and he ran into her.

c. Andrea was proud that she was prettier than Sandra. _____
_____
_____

d. Steve and Rob felt proud about being tougher than the other boys. _____
_____
_____

It is NOT peaceful to be around a PRIDEFUL person.
It IS peaceful to be around a MEEK person.

6. What does a MEEK person do? Match up the halves of the sentences to find out.

A MEEK person who wins,	will leave the biggest for someone else.
A MEEK person who loses,	will say "I'm sorry" and mean it.
A MEEK person who gets to choose a treat,	will be kind to the winners.
A MEEK person who has a chance to help someone,	will be kind to the losers.
A MEEK person who makes a mistake,	will do it without expecting anything in return.

*Have you ever been meek? Write about it on the Information Page under "One way I have been meek."

41

7. Who is the best example of meekness?

God is the <u>best</u> example of meekness. God outdoes any super hero anyone could ever invent. And the best part is, God is real. He really did create the earth. But instead of coming here to show off proudly, He chose to be meek and serve us, even die for us.

Jesus showed us what meekness does. If you have trusted Jesus as your LORD, then you have a new nature. With that new nature comes meekness. You can choose to let the meekness of your new nature make you meek.

from Katie, age 10:
"When I have to wait, I play a game or draw or get ready. I find something to do that is fun." GOOD ADVICE, KATIE!

Part B. LOYALTY

1.
"The king said to me, 'What is it you want?'
Then I prayed to the God of heaven, and I answered the king,
'If it pleases the king and if your servant has found favor in his sight,
let him send me to the city in Judah where my fathers are buried
so that I can rebuild it.'"
Nehemiah 2: 4, 5

Nehemiah showed loyalty to God by OBEYING HIS CALL TO BUILD THE WALL.
Nehemiah showed loyalty to the King by SERVING HIM FOR A TIME INSTEAD OF LEAVING EARLY FOR JERUSALEM.
Nehemiah showed loyalty to his country by RETURNING TO REBUILD THE WALL.

It is safe to say that Nehemiah was a LOYAL man.

On the Information Page, write one of the ways Nehemiah was loyal. While you are there, write about one way you have been loyal.

2. Nehemiah is not the only loyal person God talks about in the Bible. You'll see for yourself in this LOYALTY LOOK-UP. Get your Bible and a pencil ready.

Loyalty Look-up

Loyal Person	Verse to Look Up	What Happened?
Eleazar, son of Dodai the Ahohite.	2 Samuel 23:9, 10	
God	I Samuel 3:19	
Israelites	Joshua 1:17	
Joseph	Genesis 49:33-50:14	
Jesus	John 12:1-8	
Friends of Jesus	John 19: 25-27	
The Apostles	Acts 5:25-29	
Paul	Philemon 10, 11, 12, 17, 18	
Moses	Hebrews 11:24-27	

Staying true to those I serve.   **Loyalty**   Staying true only to myself.

How does loyalty look today?

3. You have seen how loyalty looked in people's lives in the Bible. How does it look in people's lives today?

This Person:	Shows Loyalty to:	In this way:
a. A husband	his wife	_____
b. A wife	her husband	_____
c. A worker	the boss	_____
d. A brother	his brother or sister	_____
e. A student	his or her school	_____
f. A friend	a friend	_____
g. A grandchild	a grandparent	_____
h. A child	his or her parents	_____
i. A citizen	his or her country	_____
j. A Christian	God	_____

4. Now that you have seen what LOYALTY looks like in people's lives, you will know how to use it when it is your turn. LOYALTY will look <u>great</u> on you!

A simple saying for you to say without your tongue twisting terribly.

Loyalty lovingly lingers, lasting longer.

WORDS ABOUT WAITING

from Barbara, age 9:
"The other day I went over to my friend's house and left my old jeans there because my Mom was going to get me some new ones. Anyway, I waited two long weeks to get some new jeans, and I still haven't gotten them!"

Part C. JOY

1. There is a lady who loves Jesus that says this about her joy:

> "When I trusted Jesus to be my Savior, He gave me a special joy. I picture my joy in Jesus as being in a pretty little box. When sadness or anger or BIG problems come along, they try to steal my little box of joy, but I won't let them. No matter how bad things get, I'm going to keep the joy that Jesus gave me when I became His child."

2. Joy is a calm smile inside of us no matter what else is going on. It is different than being happy. It is different than being excited. Of course, joy CAN make us feel happy and excited.

3. Joy comes from God. We can't get it on our own. It's a joy from Jesus.

ENJOY! REJOICE!

4. The people who rebuilt the wall found out some bad news.

They found out how far they had turned from God. This made them very sad. They were sorry for their sin and worshipped God again like they used to. But they wouldn't let go of the sadness over their sin. Nehemiah kindly helped them understand that the time for sadness was over. Now it was time to rejoice!

> "Nehemiah said, 'Go and ENJOY choice food and sweet drinks, and send some to those who have nothing prepared. This day is sacred to our LORD. Do not grieve, for the JOY of the LORD is your strength.'"
> Nehemiah 8:10

5. CAN YOU REPEAT THAT, PLEASE?

- The people found out some _____ _____.

- They found out how far they had _____ _____ _____.

- They were _____ for their sin and _____ God again like they used to.

- But they wouldn't let go of the _____ over their _____,

- Nehemiah kindly helped _____ _____ that the time for sadness was _____.

- Now it was time to _____!

- Nehemiah told them to _____

_____

_____

Feeling a deep delight in my soul.

Joy

Feeling an emptiness in my soul.

6. If you were told to celebrate God's love by eating choice foods and drinking sweet drinks, what would you order?

MY CHOICE FOR CHOICE FOODS: _____

_____

_____

MY CHOICE FOR SWEET DRINKS: _____

_____

Nehemiah told them to share their joy by sending some of their food and drinks to others. WITH WHOM WOULD YOU SHARE YOUR FOOD?

_____

_____

7. Listen to your teacher read something that God told Paul to write in the Bible. You can find it in your Bible in I Timothy 6:17. Listen for the word JOY.

What do you really ENJOY? _____

_____

8. Do you think God wants us to ENJOY our JOY? _____

Being grumpy or always wearing a long face does not mean that you are too serious about God to smile. It means that you are letting the grumps take over the joy that Jesus gave you.

JOY is POWERFUL! It is your STRENGTH!
ENJOY it!

A YOUR TURN
TWISTER
A simple saying for you to say without your tongue twisting terribly.

_____

_____

WORDS ABOUT WAITING

from Jenny, age 9:
"One day I had to wait 20 minutes for my biscuits to bake, and I was very hungry." Have you ever baked biscuits?

Waiting for Christmas

Josh, Aaron, Dean, Matthew, and Katie think it is too hard to wait for Christmas. Is that how you feel?

Katie says, "One day I got up and ate breakfast. Then I remembered that today was Christmas Eve. I couldn't wait until the next day. That day went very, very slow. While I waited for the day to end, I wrapped presents and made cards."

Katie had a good idea. ONE GOOD WAY TO HELP THE TIME UNTIL CHRISTMAS GO BY QUICKLY IS TO GET BUSY THINKING ABOUT WHAT TO GIVE OTHERS.

OUR IDEAS ABOUT
THINGS KIDS CAN <u>GIVE</u> FOR CHRISTMAS

_____

_____

_____

_____

_____

_____

_____

_____

_____

_____

Become a Christmas helper. As a gift of love to Jesus, you can show extra kindness to the people around you. Help without being asked. Clean up some messes that aren't yours. Keep the kitchen floor swept.

Watch people and pray for them. When you're waiting at the mall for Mom to finish her shopping, watch the people. Try to spot the things you have studied in this book, like obedience, wisdom, attentiveness, and meekness. Pray for some of the people you see. Ask God to give them the love and joy of Jesus.

Whatever you do, don't sit around wondering what is inside the gifts with your name on them. That's what Dean did one year and he ended up yelling because he didn't think he could wait any longer.

Merry Christmas Waiting!

Get ready to meet some young heroes in this unit. That happens after you take a look at what hot-tempers and lying can do to a person. And if you have a favorite sport season, you will be given some tips on how to wait for it to arrive.

Fill in the facts as you find them.

Self-control

Self-control means: _____

_____

God's thoughts about self-control: _____

_____

Nehemiah showed self-control by: _____

_____

One way that I have been self-controlled: _____

_____

Honesty

Honesty means: _____

_____

God's thoughts about honesty: _____

_____

Nehemiah showed honesty by: _____

_____

One way that I have been honest: _____

_____

Helpfulness

Helpfulness means: _____

_____

God's thoughts about helpfulness: _____

_____

Nehemiah showed helpfulness by: _____

_____

One way that I have been helpful: _____

_____

Nehemiah tells Jerusalem's leaders that they have done wrong.

NEHEMIAH

The Tax Problem

[a] The wall kept getting higher, but so did something else!
The taxes and the cost of food made some folks cry and yell!

[b] They came to Nehemiah, complaining of the costs.
His anger rose against the men who made them suffer loss.

[c] "You're taxing your own people. They're losing what they own.
You're doing wrong, so stop it now. Give them back their homes."

[d] The leaders and the tax men knew his words were true.
They promised to stop taxing and gave the goods back, too.

[e] The people liked his leadership and named him governor.
He led with Godly wisdom and stood up for the poor.

[f] His helpfulness showed every day. His hard work led the rest.
Nehemiah was pleasing God and doing what was best.

1. In this part of the story, who had lost control? _____

2. Do you think Nehemiah lost control when he spoke to the leaders? _____ Yes _____ No

3. What was happening among the Jews? _____

4. How were the leaders being dishonest? _____

5. On the Information Page, write one way that Nehemiah showed honesty.

6. Nehemiah's helpfulness showed in many ways. Name two of them, then choose one answer to be written on the Information Page under "One way Nehemiah showed helpfulness."

7. How have you been self-controlled this week? Write your answer on the Information Page.

Part A. SELF-CONTROL

"Do not make friends with a hot-tempered man,
do not associate with one easily angered, or you may learn his ways
and get yourself ensnared."
Proverbs 22:24

1. Explain this verse in your own words: _____

_____

_____

2. Solomon is giving you advice that he knows is true. His father, David, must have told him some true and scary stories about his days as a young man.

A Hot-Tempered Story.

David was playing the harp for King Saul, as he usually did. Saul was jealous because David had killed Goliath. He angrily hurled his spear at David, hoping to pin him to the wall.

What is one thing you have seen a hot-tempered person do? _____

Another Hot-Tempered Story.

One day King Saul threw his spear at his own son because he was David's best friend.

What is one thing you have done when your temper was hot? _____

And Another Hot-Tempered Story.

David's big brother, Eliab, got very angry with him. Turn in your Bible to I Samuel 17:26-30. Read about it, then write what each brother said:

Eliab said, "_____"

David said, "_____"

What did David do next? _____.

3. King Saul had a problem with his temper. He liked throwing spears at those people who cared for him the most. Sometimes those we love throw their anger at us, and sometimes we throw our anger at them.

Hot tempers can bring hot problems to a person's life.

A simple saying for you to say without your tongue twisting terribly.

Terrible tempers have tarnishing tendencies.

NEHEMIAH'S ANGER

4. Nehemiah found out that the leaders of Jerusalem had been taxing the people. Many people couldn't pay the taxes, and so the leaders were making them give up their homes and livestock, and even their children. Would this make you mad?
Yes _____ No _____

What would you do? _____

_____

What did Nehemiah do? _____

_____

5. When God says to be careful around hot-tempered people, does He mean that getting angry is always wrong? Yes _____ No _____ Be ready to explain your answer.

6. On the flames on this page write some things that hot-tempered people get mad about.
On the flames on page 50, write some things hot-tempered people do when they are mad.

7. What are some things a hot-tempered person doesn't get to enjoy? _____

_____

8. What about you? On the Information Page, write one way you have controlled your temper.

WORDS ABOUT WAITING

from Dean, age 9:
"Once I had to wait twenty minutes to ride on a roller coaster that I would only get to ride one time. It was worth it!"

Part B. HONESTY

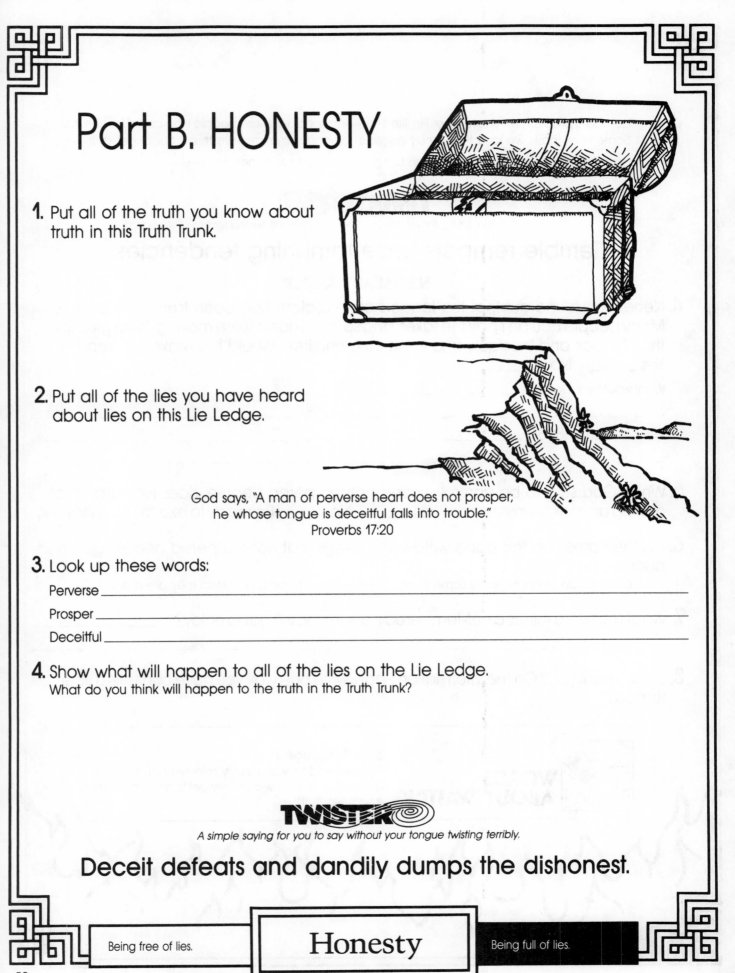

1. Put all of the truth you know about truth in this Truth Trunk.

2. Put all of the lies you have heard about lies on this Lie Ledge.

God says, "A man of perverse heart does not prosper; he whose tongue is deceitful falls into trouble."
Proverbs 17:20

3. Look up these words:

Perverse _____

Prosper _____

Deceitful _____

4. Show what will happen to all of the lies on the Lie Ledge.
What do you think will happen to the truth in the Truth Trunk?

TWISTER
A simple saying for you to say without your tongue twisting terribly.

Deceit defeats and dandily dumps the dishonest.

Being free of lies. | Honesty | Being full of lies.

5. The liar will always end up in trouble. The truth-teller will always end up in peace. That's just the way it is, because God's way always brings peace.

6. Think about the lives of the liar and the truth-teller. What kinds of things fill up the days of the liar? What kinds of things fill up the days of the truth-teller? Write your thoughts in each trail on this page.

The Life of THE LIAR　　　　　　　　　**The Life of THE TRUTH-TELLER**

TROUBLE *Peace*

Part C. HELPFULNESS

God is always helping us. He never sleeps and He is always watching over us. That is hard for us to understand. Do you think it is hard for God to understand when we have trouble helping those around us?

God asks us over and over in the Bible to show love to others. He means that we should do more than just smile at them, even though smiling is a nice thing to do. By helping those who need it, we are doing what Jesus would do if He were here.

There are many people who are obeying God and caring about others more than themselves.

HELPER #1

The homeless are being helped by one boy who cared about them and decided he would like to give them food. He asked his father to take him downtown so he could give away his food to the people who didn't have any. He said he was doing it because that's what Jesus would have done.

He went back night after night. Soon others were helping fix the food and delivering it. Then more people helped. And then the day came when his father quit his job to go to work for his son feeding the homeless. Now hundreds of people across the country are doing what this young helper did.

HELPER #2

A little girl who had cancer was helped by her brother. He couldn't do much, but he did find one way to help. He swam! People had promised to pay him money for every lap he swam. He swam 250 laps (almost 3½ miles) and earned $30,000. He gave the money to some doctors who are working to find out how to cure cancer.

HELPER #3

A boy who was burned badly all over his body was helped by the love of a friend. The boy didn't look the same anymore, and people usually looked the other way or stared when he walked by. But his friend didn't. Instead, he spent time playing and eating and talking with his friend who had suffered so much from the burns. He knew that under the burned skin, his friend was still the same person he had always liked. After all, bodies are just like shells holding the <u>real</u> us inside them.

HELPER #4: YOU

What will you do to make a difference? _____

_____

_____

A YOUR TURN

A simple saying for you to say without your tongue twisting terribly.

_____

_____

| Doing what I can for someone else. | Helpfulness | Ignoring the needs of others. |

I lift up my _____ to the _____ — where does my help come from? My help comes from the Lord, the Maker of _____ and _____. He will not let your _____ slip — He who watches over you will not slumber; indeed, He who watches over Israel will neither slumber nor _____.

Psalm 121:1-4

Waiting for a Sports Season

Charlene says: "I hate waiting! But I try. And I do wait. Like for basketball season to come. Like now, soccer season just started and I hate soccer or I would play. But I have to wait for basketball."

Kristen says: "I have been in the JC Relays for two years. I have trouble waiting for them to get here each year."

Matt, age 9, says: "I always wanted to play basketball. Sometimes I get a little impatient to play basketball. So I started to think of soccer and played it, too."

Josh, age 8, says: "When soccer was over, I missed it, but to be patient I did other fun things that I like, like riding my skateboard and reading a good book."

Aaron, age 8, says: "I had to practice and practice and practice some more for soccer and buy stuff like soccer balls and cleats. And also I had to read the rules. And now it is time! Boy! Was I impatient!"

Tony, age 9, says: "I bought a baseball, and my brother and I played baseball. It was just like the sport season was here. And then we went to watch a semi-pro game."

1. What is your favorite sport? _____

2. Which of the athletes on this page seem the wisest while waiting for their favorite sport season to begin?

_____

_____

_____

3. What will you do to wait wisely this season?

Want another clue that God is real? Just think about the way your muscles are connected to help you move during your favorite sport! Muscles are no accident.

Congratulations! You have diligently finished five units of this book. And you did it just in time to celebrate with Nehemiah, who also finished something. Patience and dependability will help you make it through this unit to the next one. Also, a short visit to the Waiting Room will help you learn how to wait for help.

Fill in the facts as you find them.

Diligence

Diligence means: _____

_____

God's thoughts about diligence: _____

_____

Nehemiah showed diligence by: _____

_____

One way that I have been diligent: _____

_____

Patience

Patience means: _____

_____

God's thoughts about patience: _____

_____

Nehemiah showed patience by: _____

_____

One way that I have been patient: _____

_____

Dependability

Dependability means: _____

_____

God's thoughts about dependability: _____

_____

Nehemiah showed dependability by: _____

_____

One way that I have been dependable: _____

_____

Sanballat and Tobiah's mocking is stilled when they see the wall that the people finished with God's help.

NEHEMIAH

The Unsuccessful Bluff

[a]One day there came a message which sounded nice enough.
But Nehemiah knew that it was nothing but a bluff.

[b]Sanballat and Tobiah, the senders of the note,
were asking for a meeting at a place that was remote.

[c]Nehemiah knew the two still wanted him to die.
He told them he would not be there and also told them why.

[d]"The project needs me here, you know. Why should I leave it now?"
His answer didn't please them and they itched to knock him out.

[e]Four times they tried it. Four times he didn't show.
Four times Nehemiah said, "Oh no" to Ono.

[f]The last try was a dirty trick. The message held a lie.
But Nehemiah called their bluff and blew the lie sky high.

1. How did Nehemiah know that the message was a bluff? _____

2. Sanballat and Tobiah were diligent in doing wrong. What is one wrong they had done? _____
_____

3. Would you have gone to the Plain of Ono to meet Sanballat and Tobiah? ____ Yes ____ No Why?
_____

4. The people depended on Nehemiah. What is one way he was dependable? Write your answer on the Information Page.

5. Who depends on you? _____

   How are you most dependable? _____

6. What part of Nehemiah's job do you think took the most patience? _____
_____

7. How have you shown patience at home? Write your answer on the Information Page.

Part A. DILIGENCE

A simple saying for you to say without your tongue twisting terribly.

Finally finishing feels fabulous!

1. What are some of your "fabulous finishes"?

_____
_____
_____
_____

Give yourself a grin for each fabulous finish on your list.
If your list is empty, don't despair. You're about to finish something – this page!

2. Pretend this verse about Nehemiah's fabulous finish is part of a story in a newspaper.
Print a headline of your choice above it:

JUDAEAN TIMES

25¢

PUBLISHED DAILY BY THE KING'S PRESS   NEHEMIAH 6:15, 16

all our enemies heard about this and all the surrounding

New Wall at 4th and Well St.

nations saw it, our enemies lost their self-confidence, because they realized that this work had been done with the help of our God."

JUDAH – "So the wall was completed on the twenty-fifth of Elul, in fifty-two days. When

3. Both Nehemiah and his enemies were diligent. But Nehemiah was diligent in doing
_____ and his enemies were diligent in doing _____ .

Doing my work steadily until it is done.	**Diligence**	Quitting when I feel like it.

60

4. Name two of the ways Sanballat and Tobiah were diligent in trying to keep the wall from being rebuilt.

a. _____

_____

b. _____

_____

Name two of the ways Nehemiah was diligent in getting the wall rebuilt.

c. _____

_____

d. _____

_____

Now, write one of these on the Information Page under "One way Nehemiah was diligent."

5. Your opinion, please.

a. Would God have chosen Nehemiah to lead the wall project if Nehemiah had not been diligent?   YES   NO

b. Would you have chosen Nehemiah to lead the wall project if he had not been diligent?   YES   NO

c. Could the people have finished the wall in 52 days without God's help?   YES   NO

d. Did God enjoy helping the people rebuild the wall?   YES   NO

e. Do you believe there are people today who are diligent like Nehemiah?   YES   NO

f. Do you believe there are people today who make fun of people who are serving God diligently?   YES   NO

g. Do you believe God still helps people get things done?   YES   NO

h. Do you believe God is diligent in helping the diligent?   YES   NO

THANK YOU FOR YOUR OPINION.

6. You are with grown-ups every day. Some of them are diligent. Some of them are not.

Do you think the grown-ups who are not diligent wanted to turn out that way? What happened? How can you keep it from happening to you?

NEHEMIAH WAS WILLING TO WAIT FOR THE RIGHT TIME TO REBUILD THE WALL.
WHEN HE GETS TO HEAVEN, WILL HE SAY IT WAS WORTH THE WAIT?

7. Say the DILIGENCE TWISTER 52 times in honor of the 52 days it took to finish the wall. Doesn't finishing feel fabulous?

WORDS ABOUT WAITING

from Dean:
"I waited one whole day before I could get out of our car on our trip to Colorado." Was Colorado worth the wait? Of course!

Part B. PATIENCE

1. Patiently copy the words from Proverbs 15:18 onto these lines:

_____

_____

_____

2. In this verse, the hot-tempered man "stirs up _____."
Look up "dissension" in your dictionary. What does it mean?

_____

_____

Does it sound like something you would enjoy being around? Yes_____ No_____

3. In the same verse, what does the patient man do? "The patient man _____
_____ _____."
Look up "calm" in your dictionary. What does it mean?

_____

_____

Does it sound like something you would enjoy being around? Yes_____ No_____

JUST THINK! By learning to be a patient person
you would be a portable calming machine.

TWISTER

A simple saying for you to say without your tongue twisting terribly.

Patience perseveres past pesky problems.

4. Here are some pesky problems. How might patience persevere past them? Read
through the list, then WAIT for your teacher's directions.

   a. Gerald's father is upset after finding the cat on his bed again.

   b. Shannon's sister is blaming Shannon for losing her newest earring by knocking it
      off the dresser.

   c. Taking out the garbage is Scott's job. It tipped over on the kitchen floor.

   d. Joni just used the last of the milk for her cereal just as Ron reached for it to pour
      it on his cereal.

| Choosing to wait with calmness. | Patience | Letting anger rule my waiting. |

5. There is a famous story about King Solomon and two mothers who were quarrelling over a baby boy. It is written in I Kings 3:16-28. Listen as your teacher reads it to you, then write the main events of the story on these story blocks.

WOMAN #1 SAID:	WOMAN #1 SAID:

WOMAN #2 SAID:	WOMAN #2 SAID:

THE KING SAID:	THE KING SAID:

6. Solomon mixed _____ and _____ with _____ to calm this quarrel.

WORDS ABOUT WAITING

from Jeanah, age 9:
"Once I was at the dentist's office. I was waiting for the dentist to come out and tell me if I had to have a retainer. He finally came out and said, 'No!'"

Part C. DEPENDABILITY

1. Hezekiah was a man you could count on. Who do you know that you can count on?

_____

2. God says that:
"In everything that he undertook in the service of God's temple and in obedience to the law and the commands, he sought his God and worked wholeheartedly. And so he prospered."

Why did he prosper? _____

3. If you think prospering sounds like a good idea, should you work WHOLEHEARTEDLY or HALF-HEARTEDLY in serving God and doing the work you have to do? Circle your choice.

Being trusted to keep my word.

Dependability

Going back on my word.

4. How could these jobs be done wholeheartedly? How could they be done half-heartedly? Fill in the chart with your ideas.

—— THE JOB	WHOLEHEARTEDLY	HALFHEARTEDLY
Carrying groceries		
Mowing lawns		
Cooking food		
Sewing clothes		
Washing dishes		
Repairing motors		
Going to school		
Driving a truck		
Being a friend		
Being a parent		
Being a son or daughter		

A YOUR TURN

TWISTER

A simple saying for you to say without your tongue twisting terribly.

Being trusted to keep my word.

Dependability

Going back on my word.

Here's another batch of hidden words. This time the bonus word is in the puzzle but not on the list. If you want a hint, look at the bottom of this page.

```
S E L F C O N T R O L B M N O I F P
M M B V D I L I G E N C E R R L M R
U Z X C V B N A S N E G N E K L P I
G Q W E R T P E T J O Y J O Y R L D
H H K M I U R I Y O O O O U L P X E
D E P E N D A B I L I T Y R Y I I E
U T H E U B D E C C H R I S T M A S
Y B H K E E A E E K V B N E L M N M
F U L N V C X E E C N E I T A P X W
H O N E S T Y U X V B N M Y Y K I U
E Y T S H J K U I K J Y U O O L I Y
N N S S E N L U F P L E H O L I D E
```

Meekness   Patience
Loyalty   Dependability
Joy   Pride
Self control   Smug
Honesty   Enjoy
Helpfulness   Rejoice
Diligence

(The word is a special day that happens in December)

Waiting for Help

Have you ever had to wait a long time for someone to help you out of danger?

_____

One day in September of 1985 a big earthquake hit Mexico City. A man named Jose was trapped underneath the hospital where he worked. He WAITED for help for two days and 23 hours. Many other people waited even longer.

In THE WAITING ROOM today, you will be learning how to wait for help when you are in danger.

WHEN I AM IN DANGER AND NEED HELP I WILL:

THINK SMARTLY
   Our ideas about thinking smartly: _____
   _____
   _____

WAIT CALMLY
   Our ideas about waiting calmly: _____
   _____
   _____

TRUST FULLY
   Our ideas about trusting fully: _____
   _____
   _____

A prayer for when we are in danger.
Dear God,
Please _____
_____
_____

Three of the hardest things for us to do are **(1)** saying "sorry," **(2)** being fair, and **(3)** liking people who are different than we are. But just because something is tough doesn't mean we can't do it. Lots of great people are forgiving, fair, and tolerant. You'll meet them in this unit!

Fill in the facts as you find them.

Forgiveness

Forgiveness means: _____

_____

God's thoughts about forgiveness: _____

_____

Nehemiah showed forgiveness by: _____

_____

One way that I have been forgiving: _____

_____

Fairness

Fairness means: _____

_____

God's thoughts about fairness: _____

_____

Nehemiah showed fairness by: _____

_____

One way that I have been fair: _____

_____

Tolerance

Tolerance means: _____

_____

God's thoughts about tolerance: _____

_____

Nehemiah showed tolerance by: _____

_____

One way that I have been tolerant: _____

_____

Nehemiah's good idea ended with a happy celebration.

NEHEMIAH

The Finish

^aThe building crew kept working hard, and soon the wall was finished. When Sanballat and Tobiah heard, their sneers and jeers dimished.

^bGod had helped them build the wall and everybody knew it. Fifty-two days is all it took to totally redo it.

^cOn the wall the guards and keepers gladly stood in place. Pleased that they no longer were the object of disgrace.

^dThe gladness wasn't over. There was much more yet to come. But first a giant sadness fell over everyone.

^eThe God who helped them build the wall did it out of love. But they had never loved Him back or cared what He had done.

^fWhen Ezra read God's Word to them, they cried about their sin. Then God forgave the wrong they did and gave them joy again.

1. Nehemiah had to choose guards and leaders to be in charge of the wall. If you were choosing guards and leaders, how would your decide fairly who should do what? _____
   _____
   _____

2. How long did it take the people to rebuild the wall? _____ days

3. Did Tobiah's words in the story in Unit Four come true?   Yes ___ No ___
   What were his words? _____

4. What caused the giant sadness that came over everyone? _____
   How did they get over their sadness? _____

5. How long did the people stand to hear God's Word? _____
   We are used to having Bibles with us, but there are many people in the world who would gladly stand all day to hear God's Word. Whose words are more important than God's?
   _____

6. Hundreds of families had worked together on the wall. They had many differences. Name three ways that families who worked together would need to show tolerance:
   _____
   _____
   _____

7. How does our wonderful God show tolerance? _____
   _____
   _____

Part A. FORGIVENESS

A simple saying for you to say without your tongue twisting terribly.

Saying "sorry" isn't silly.

1. Some people believe that saying "sorry" IS silly. They don't like admitting they have done wrong. God says:

> "Fools mock at making amends for sin,
> but good will is found among the upright."
> Proverbs 14:9

2. Replace-A-Word. Here are some words that mean the same as five of the words in the verse. Choose the ones you like best to say the same thing another way.

Mock	Amends	Sin	Good Will	Upright
Ridicule	Correcting	Doing wrong	Peacefulness	The honorable
Sneer about	Making up for	Evil	Kindness	Those that do right
Joke about	Apologizing for	Wickedness	Understanding	The just

"Fools _____,

but _____ is found among _____."

3. "We're Sorry!"

After the wall was finished, the people of Jerusalem asked Ezra to read the part of the Bible God had given to Moses. What they heard made them understand that they had been ignoring God and doing wrong. This made them very sorry and full of shame.

They cried and told God about all the wrong they had done. They wrote promises to God about doing right, and everyone signed the promise note. The Jerusalem people wanted forgiveness from God.

Do you think God forgave them?   Yes ___ No ___   What makes you think so?

4. "I'm Sorry!"

Have you ever made a mistake?   Yes ___ No ___

Have you ever done wrong on purpose?   Yes ___ No ___

Everyone who has ever lived, except _____, has made mistakes and has done wrong on purpose. EVERYONE. But not everyone has said, "I'm sorry" to God or others.

a. What do you think would keep a person from saying "I'm sorry" to God?

_____

b. What do you think would keep a person from saying "I'm sorry" to others?

_____

_____

c. Think about a time when you said "I'm sorry" to God or someone else. What happened? Write on the Information Page under, "One time that I asked for forgiveness."

Caring more about God than my grudge.	Forgiveness	Caring more about my grudge than about God.

5. Making Amends.

a. On somebody's street in somebody's town, somebody's Dad did this:

- He got out of bed, got dressed and ate breakfast.
- He went outside to mow the lawn with a mower he borrowed from his neighbor.
- He pushed the mower over a small pile of leaves.
- The rock under the small pile of leaves broke the blade of the mower.
- He turned the mower off and took it back to the neighbor's garage. But he didn't tell anyone what had happened.
- The next morning the neighbor got out of bed, got dressed and ate breakfast.
- He went outside to mow his lawn. *What happened next?*

- _____
- _____
- _____
- The men were still neighbors, but they stopped being friends.

b. On the list you just read, place an arrow by the sentence that tells you the blade broke. Rewrite the rest of the story by showing one way the man could have made amends for breaking the mower.

- _____
- _____
- _____
- _____
- _____
- _____
- _____

c. Some grown-ups have never learned to say "I'm sorry." Others have learned to say "I'm sorry," but have never learned to make amends. Their lives have spots of anger and sadness because of it. If you learn to apologize and make amends while you are young, your life will have peace in place of the spots of anger or sadness.

6. Here's what I'd do. Fill in this chart with words and actions that show how to say "I'm sorry" and make amends.

The mistake or the wrong	Words to use in saying "sorry"	Amends to make
I broke the neighbor's gate		
I stole money from Uncle John		
I lost a friend's book		
I opened my sister's mail		
I told my friend's secret to another friend and now everyone knows the secret.		

71

Remember, everyone makes mistakes and sometimes does wrong on purpose. But, not everyone is wise enough to say "I'm sorry" or try to make amends. Are you?

WORDS ABOUT WAITING

from Matthew, age 9:
"One time I couldn't wait to hear the next part of a story." What is the best story that has ever been read to you: _____

_____

Part B. FAIRNESS

1. Many people say, "That's not fair!" to many kinds of things. When do YOU hear, "That's not fair"?

   a. On the playground: _____

   b. In class: _____

   c. At home: _____

   d. On the news: _____

2. Here is one thing God says is not fair: Treating rich people better than poor people.

"My brothers, as believers in our glorious LORD Jesus Christ, don't show favoritism. Suppose a man comes into your meeting wearing a gold ring and fine clothes, and a poor man in shabby clothes also comes in. If you show special attention to the man wearing fine clothes and say, 'Here's a good seat for you,' but say to the poor man, 'You can stand there,' or 'Sit on the floor by my feet,' have you not discriminated among yourselves and become judges with evil thoughts?"
James 2:1-4

3. Be ready to talk about:

   a. The events of this story.

   b. The feelings of the two men in this story.

   c. The reasons we sometimes treat rich people better than poor people.

   d. Ways to show fairness to the rich and the poor.

| Judging a situation correctly. | **Fairness** | Showing favorites in my decisions. |

4. My Fairness Story

In your mind, pretend that you are standing at the door of a church the day a rich man and a poor man come to the meeting. What happens? Write it here:

_____

_____

_____

_____

_____

_____

_____

_____

_____

_____

_____

_____

_____

_____

_____

_____

_____

_____

_____

_____

_____

_____

TWISTER

A simple saying for you to say without your tongue twisting terribly.

Faulty fairness fosters feuding.

5. Why does unfairness make people mad? _____

6. Do you think unfairness upsets God? _____

7. Which kind of unfairness upsets you the most? _____

_____

WORDS ABOUT WAITING

from Jeff, age 9:
"When I went to Disneyland, I had to wait to ride on the Thunder Mountain Railroad." DO YOU THINK JEFF WAS GLAD HE WAITED?

_____

Part C. TOLERANCE

1. Look at the bottom of the page and read the meaning of TOLERANCE. What are some of the differences you and your classmates have noticed in people?

Differences I Have Noticed in People

_____

_____

_____

_____

_____

_____

_____

_____

_____

_____

_____

_____

_____

_____

_____

_____

_____

_____

_____

_____

2. Differences can often cause anger. But living happily together even if we have differences can bring peace and joy. Tolerance of our differences is wise. God says: "How good and pleasant it is when brothers live together in unity." Psalm 133:1

3. There are many people who have learned tolerance. They are pleasant to be with. One Mom and Dad were so tolerant of others that they did something that must have brought a smile to the heart of God. Doris Lund wrote about it in a book called PATCHWORK CLAN. Your public library may have it on one of its shelves.

| Accepting the differences of others. | Tolerance | Mocking the differences of others. |

One True Story of Tolerance

[a] Ann and John Sweeney were Mom and Dad to five children, and they were excited about the sixth one that was on the way. But the baby died before it was born, and the family felt very sad. They would miss being with this member of their family.

[b] Since they were parents whose child couldn't be with them, they decided to adopt a child who couldn't be with his parents. They chose red-haired Marcus. Some of his relatives were American Indians, and some of them were Blacks.

[c] Later, the family was surprised when Mom gave birth to twins! They were having such a good time growing as a family that after the twins were born, John and Ann adopted two MORE children. Their names were Faith and Terry. (How many were in the family now?)

[d] Next, they invited a teenager from Vietnam and a blind Colombian Indian girl to come and live with them.

[e] Also chosen along the way were Chuong, Huong, and Dat, three children from Vietnam. They had climbed into a crowded boat that was escaping Vietnam, but the boat left too quickly for their parents to get on the boat with them. Chuong was left to care for his baby sister, Huong, and his little brother, Dat.

[f] Chuong kept thinking back to that scary day. The Sweeneys were patient with him. Their love and kindness helped him with his sadness. It even helped him know how to show patience and kindness to two new brothers the family adopted from a New York ghetto. Their names were Carey and Michael.

[g] It wasn't easy for different people to live in the same house. They had fights and messes and big problems. But they worked them out together – with love and tolerance.

What do you think is the reason the book about the Sweeneys is called PATCHWORK CLAN?

Something to think about. We can see that the Sweeneys are tolerant people by the things they did. Think about other ways we can tell if a person is tolerant.

A YOUR TURN

A simple saying for you to say without your tongue twisting terribly.

Waiting for a Turn

Daniel doesn't like waiting for the light to change when he's in a hurry to get to his basketball game. Sarah gets tired of waiting to ask her teacher a question. Where and when do you and your friends wait for turns?

_____

_____

_____

_____

_____

Waiting for a turn is another part of life that just happens. There is no way to get rid of having to wait for a turn.

So what can we do about it?

GROUP 1
We can grumble and complain.
We can snarl and gripe.
We can honk horns and shout.
We can glare and frown.

OUR CHOICES

GROUP 2
We can talk to God.
We can think about a happy memory.
We can tell ourselves a joke.
We can smile at someone
or say a kind word.

The results of our choices

What types of things happen
when we choose from Group 1?

What types of things happen
when we choose from Group 2?

_____   _____

_____   _____

Which group of choices do you think God would recommend?   GROUP 1   GROUP 2
Which group of choices do you recommend?   GROUP 1   GROUP 2

Be ready to talk about:
1. Something you might say to God while waiting your turn.
2. A happy memory you have in your mind.
3. A favorite joke.
4. A time you smiled or said a kind word to someone while waiting.

Good ideas are like popcorn. They pop here and there in our minds and can be a tasty addition to life. Catching the popping ideas and serving them to others will bring you great joy. God is interested in your ideas, so keep them popping. You'll learn how to do that in this unit.

Fill in the facts as you find them.

Initiative

Initiative means: _____

_____

God's thoughts about initiative: _____

_____

Nehemiah showed initiative by: _____

_____

One way that I have shown initiative: _____

_____

Love

Love means: _____

_____

God's thoughts about love: _____

_____

Nehemiah showed love by: _____

_____

One way that I have shown love: _____

_____

Resourcefulness

Resourcefulness means: _____

_____

God's thoughts about resourcefulness: _____

_____

Nehemiah showed resourcefulness by: _____

_____

One way that I have been resourceful: _____

_____

The people stood all day as Ezra read the words of God.

NEHEMIAH

The Good-Idea Parade

ᵃNehemiah's good ideas helped him get things done.
He organized the people and cared for everyone.

ᵇOne good idea he thought of brought music to the land.
He planned a celebration led by a marching band.

ᶜThe singers and the leaders led the large promenade.
They marched on top the rebuilt wall in a praise the Lord parade.

ᵈThey talked and praised and sang to God as one big happy throng.
They knew that He was there with them, pleased to hear their song.

ᵉTime went by, and Nehemiah went back to the king.
He chose good men to watch the wall and every little thing.

ᶠThings were far from perfect, but Nehemiah knew
that God had liked his good idea and helped a dream come true.

1. How did Nehemiah show initiative in this part of the story? Write your answer on the Information Page.

2. What is your best idea of the day? _____
   What is the best idea you think you have ever had? _____

3. What resources did Nehemiah have to plan the celebration? _____
   _____

4. How did Nehemiah show love to the people? _____
   How did Nehemiah show love to God? _____
   Choose one of these answers to write on the Information Page.

5. Spend some time thinking about the celebration. Pretend you hear the music and see the singers and leaders on the wall. Are things quiet or lively? Are the people having fun, or are they wishing they were somewhere else? On another sheet of paper, write a short story pretending that you are a singer, a harpist, or a leader at the celebration. Make it sound like you are really there.

6. How can you show love to someone who is depending on you today? _____
   _____

7. Of all the ideas Nehemiah had, which one do you think was the smartest? _____
   _____

Part A. INITIATIVE

1. Our study of Nehemiah began with one good idea. Read this verse and then circle his good idea.

> "The king said to me, 'What is it you want?'
> Then I prayed to the God of Heaven, and I answered the king,
> 'If it pleases the king and if your servant has found favor in his sight,
> let him send me to the city in Judah where my fathers are buried so that
> I can rebuild it.'"
> Nehemiah 2:4,5

2. Circle the part of the verse that shows Nehemiah's trust in God.

3. Asking God for help with our ideas is very wise. If you are a child of God, you can trust Him to help you with your ideas.

Trying new ideas is nothing to be afraid of. Scientists keep trying to find cures for diseases. Athletes keep trying to _____ _____. Musicians keep trying to _____ _____ _____ _____. Seeing new ideas fail, happens to most people with good ideas. But they keep trying.

Here's a Good-Idea Formula:

THINK! PRAY! TRY!

Repeat until you're sure it will work.

4. By the time children are in fourth grade, some of them stop trying to carry out their good ideas. Don't stop! No matter what, don't stop! In fact, why don't you try to <u>double</u> your ideas?

A simple saying for you to say without your tongue twisting terribly.

Ideally, I'd double my daily ideas.

GOD'S GOOD IDEAS

5. What are some of the ideas you and your class think are God's best ideas?

_____

_____

_____

_____

_____

_____

| Carrying an idea from my mind into reality. | Initiative | Letting others get things started. |

PEOPLE'S GOOD IDEAS

6. The best ideas are the kind that help other people. What are some of the ideas you and your class think are people's best ideas?

_____

_____

_____

_____

_____

_____

_____

YOUR GOOD IDEAS

7. What are some of the ideas you and your class have thought of for helping others?

_____

_____

_____

_____

_____

Greg's Greenery

[a] A young boy named Greg Schafer lived in a town by the ocean. He used his good ideas to help others and earn money for himself at the same time.

[b] First, he sorted through the ideas in his mind. Then he chose the one that seemed best to him: growing and selling plants. He asked God's help in making the idea work.

[c] Greg asked his parents to drive him to the big city nearby to buy some plants from a plant dealer at a low price. He promised to pay his mom and dad for their time and gas as soon as he earned enough money.

[d] Next, Greg got the porch ready to be a plant store. He made shelves and price tags and filled water cans and spray bottles. He bought a sales receipt book and made a money tray out of a box. He wanted his plants to look nicer than the ones in the stores, so he covered the pots with pretty paper.

[e] Soon there was a sign in his front yard that said "Greg's Greenery." Customers liked Greg's plant store and told their friends about it. When he had earned enough money, he paid his parents back for their time and gas and even put an ad in the newspaper.

[f] Greg's idea worked. His customers liked buying plants at low prices, and Greg earned the money he needed.

[g] Some people think that kids don't have ideas that can really work. That's what they think! Which of your good ideas are you going to let people see?

8. Remember the formula? Write it here: _____

_____

_____

_____

 **WORDS ABOUT WAITING**

from Joshua:
"When I go fishing I can wait hours for a fish to bite!"

Part B. LOVE

 TWISTER

A simple saying for you to say without your tongue twisting terribly.

Love leaves a lovely luster.

1. Luster means: _____

2. Down the street from Sally's house, a grandpa tripped and fell.
His head was cut and a muscle in his leg was hurting. Some children saw him fall. One boy ran for help, another one ran to the nearest house to get a blanket, and the rest of the children stayed with him to give him comfort. Their love and kindness left a lovely _____ on the life of that grandpa.

3. Sam was playing basketball in his driveway when his neighbor, Mrs. Brock, came home from shopping for groceries.
He had just finished his thirteenth lay-up when he noticed that some money had fallen out of her purse. Sam walked over and picked it up. "Twenty dollars!" he whispered. He wanted twenty dollars, but he followed wisdom's advice and took it to her. His honesty left a lovely _____ on her life – and on his.

4. God says: "Love does no harm to its neighbor." What acts of love have left their luster in your neighborhood? _____
_____
_____

5. Jesus left a lovely luster when He lived on earth. What are some of your favorite ways He showed love to His neighbors? _____
_____
_____

6. God's love will shine on His children forever in Heaven. Heaven will be a safe and peaceful place to live. No harm or danger will frighten us, and no one will hurt us.
Name three things you will be able to do in heaven that you can't do here because of the dangers of living on earth?

a. _____

b. _____

c. _____

Caring strongly for a person or thing.	Love	Not caring about a person or thing.

Let your good ideas leave a lovely luster of love.

**WORDS ABOUT WAITING**

from Lisa, age 9:
"I think it is hard to wait for a time to think and for a chance to go to the library to read a book." Lisa seems to be a girl who likes to use her
_____ _____ _____ _____.

Part C. RESOURCEFULNESS

1. The first 8 letters in RESOURCEFULNESS spell ___ ___ ___ ___ ___ ___ ___ ___.

2. Look up the meaning of that eight-letter word that you just spelled. Does it mean:
  a. an ability
  b. a tool
  c. a strength
  d. a supply
  e. all of these

3. The next three letters almost spell what word? ___ ___ ___ ___.

4. It could be said, then, that a person with resourcefulness was ___ ___ ___ ___ of ___ ___ ___ ___ ___ ___ ___ ___.

5. What Resources?
  a. What resources does a carpenter have to attach two boards? _____
  b. What resources does a writer have to put words on a paper? _____
  c. What resources did Nehemiah have to rebuild the wall? _____
  d. What resources does a gardener have to make a yard look nice? _____
  _____
  e. What resources does an artist have to paint a picture? _____
  f. What resources does a pro basketball player have to play well? _____
  _____
  g. What resources did Shadrach, Meshach, and Abednego have to face the blazing furnace? _____
  _____
  h. What resources do car makers have to make cars? _____
  _____
  i. What resources does a child of God have to live God's way? _____
  _____
  j. What resources does God have to help you? _____
  _____

Meeting a need creatively.   **Resourcefulness**   Giving up easily.

6. God says: "Commit to the Lord whatever you do, and your plans will succeed
Proverbs 16:3

7. Could a child of God say that God is their greatest resource? Yes ____ No ____
Be ready to explain your answer.

8. a. Think back to one of your good ideas. What resources do you already <u>have</u> to complete your idea?

_____

_____

_____

_____

_____

b. What resources do you <u>need</u> to complete your idea? How can you get the resources to complete your idea?

Resources I Need	**Ways I Can Get Them**
_____	_____
_____	_____
_____	_____

9. A Quick Quiz
What resources do you have to help someone:
   a. who is lost?_____
   b. who has had a heart attack? _____
   c. who wants to know about God? _____
   d. who is hungry?_____
   e. who is lonely? _____
   f. who is embarrassed?_____

10. Your Choice:
   a. You can become a person with good ideas who uses the resources you have to get the idea done.
   b. You can become a person who thinks good ideas but never <u>does</u> them.
   c. You can let your ideas and resources go to waste.

What is your choice? a. _____ b. _____ c. _____

11. Write a TWISTER about being resourceful.

A YOUR TURN

TWISTER

A simple saying for you to say without your tongue twisting terribly.

_____

_____

Waiting for a Vacation

Summer vacation is almost here. Many of you have said that waiting for summer takes lots of patience. Others of you said that waiting for <u>any</u> vacation takes a lot of patience.

David, age 8, says: "One day I came to the dinner table. My mom said, 'David, we're going to Canada in two months.' 'WOW!' I said, 'but why did you tell me now? I'll have to wait so long.' That night I dreamt all about the trip. A few days later, my dad started packing. I asked him why. He said, 'Mom was teasing you. We're leaving today.'

David's waiting was cut short by a Mom who understood that waiting is hard work. Moms can't always do what David's did, though.

My Waiting-for-a-Vacation Story

_____

_____

_____

_____

There are many things a person can do to help themselves wait for a vacation. Three ideas are written for you on this list. You and the class will fill in the other four ideas.

Ten Ways to Wait for a Vacation

1. Make a list of things you want to do to get ready for your vacation. If you'll be hiking on your vacation, plan an exercise program to get yourself ready.

2. Study about the area you'll be visiting. Write to the Information Center and ask them to send you their Information Packet. It is usually free.

3. If it's summer vacation you are waiting for, the time will pass more quickly if you make each day before vacation as good and successful as it can be.

4. _____

5. _____

6. _____

7. _____

THE BEST VACATION OF ALL WILL START WHEN WE LEAVE FOR HEAVEN.
God has things planned for us that Disneyworld never thought of!

You've spent many months in the pages of this book. Now it's almost time to close it for the year. These last few pages will help you look back on what you've learned and look ahead to what you want to become. What you choose to become is up to you. Aim your life in God's direction. He's WAITING to help you make your life count. What are you WAITING for?

Waiting Wrap-up

TWISTER

NEHEMIAH

The Waiting Room

WORDS ABOUT WAITING

A simple saying for you to say without your tongue twisting terribly.

Waiting willingly warmly wows.

How many TWISTERS can you remember? Fill in the missing words of each TWISTER in this book.

UNIT 1: a. We welcome w___ __ __ __ __ while w___ __ __ __ __ w___ __ __ __ __.

b. D ___ __ __ __ __ __ __ definitely doesn't d___ __ __ __ __.

UNIT 2: a. L___ __ __ __ __ __ __ __ learn lasting L__ __ __ __ __ __.

b. F__ __ __ __-f __ __ __ __ __ __ f__ __ __ __ __ __ __ __ are f __ __ __

of f __ __ __ __ __ __.

UNIT 3: a. G___ __ __ __ __ __ God with gladly g___ __ __ __ __ g___ __ __ __.

b. P___ __ __ __ __ __ __ placed p___ __ __ __ __ __ __ __ __ __ profoundly

p. __ __ __ __ __.

UNIT 4: a. The s___ __ __ surely swagger to a s___ __ __ __ stumble.

b. L___ __ __ __ __ __ __ lovingly lingers, lasting L__ __ __ __ __ __.

UNIT 5: a. T___ __ __ __ __ __ __ __ t___ __ __ __ __ __ have tarnishing tendencies.

b. Deceit d___ __ __ __ __ __ and dandily d___ __ __ __ the d___ __ __ __ __ __ __ __.

UNIT 6: a. Finally f___ __ __ __ __ __ __ __ feels f___ __ __ __ __ __ __.

b. P___ __ __ __ __ __ __ perseveres past p___ __ __ __ problems.

UNIT 7: a. Saying "s___ __ __ __" isn't s___ __ __ __.

b. Faulty f___ __ __ __ __ __ __ __ f___ __ __ __ __ __ feuding.

UNIT 8: a. Ideally, I'd d___ __ __ __ __ my daily i___ __ __ __.

b. L__ __ __ leaves a lovely L___ __ __ __ __ __.

UNIT 9: a. W___ __ __ __ __ __ willingly warmly w___ __ __.

The Ten Toughest Twisters
Say the TWISTERS to yourself, then rank the ten toughest.

Top Toughies:

1. _____ 6. _____

2. _____ 7. _____

3. _____ 8. _____

4. _____ 9. _____

5. _____ 10. _____

"Delight yourself in the LORD and He will give you
the desires of your heart." Psalm 37:4

WORDS ABOUT WAITING

In this book you have read the WAITING WORDS of many kids your age. What do kids and grown-ups around you think about waiting?

Make up a few questions and tell folks you meet that you are gathering data for a paper about waiting. Ask them the questions, then write down their answers on notepaper. Sort through all of your answers. Choose four of the best, and write them on this page. Be ready to read your choices to the class.

1. The Question: _____
   WAITING WORDS
   from _____
   _____
   _____

2. The Question: _____
   WAITING WORDS
   from _____
   _____
   _____

3. The Question: _____
   WAITING WORDS
   from _____
   _____
   _____

4. The Question: _____
   WAITING WORDS
   from _____
   _____
   _____

"Commit your way to the LORD; trust in Him and He will do this: He will make your righteousness shine like the dawn, the justice of your cause like the noonday sun."
Psalm 37: 5, 6

My Early Ideas About Waiting

1. Three things I wait for the most: a. _____

　　b. _____　　　c. _____

2. Three things I think grown-ups wait for the most: a. _____

　　b. _____　　　c. _____

3. I become the most angry when I wait for _____

4. The person I know who waits best is _____

Read THE WAITING LIST. Choose one thing from the list that you have had to wait for, then write about it.

THE WAITING LIST

A special day (what kind?)	A test to be handed back
Visitors	Cement to dry
Paint to dry	Allowance to be received
Plants to grow	A new store to open
A vacation	A prize
A friend to call	A ride
Hair to grow out	A pet
A new adventure	The mail

My choice from the list: _____

Here's what happened:

_____

_____

_____

_____

_____

_____

_____

_____

_____

_____

FILL THIS IN DURING WAITING WRAP-UP:

Read what you wrote during the mini-unit. Place a mark by the answers that would
be different if you answered them now.

*"Be still before the LORD and wait patiently for Him; do not fret
when men succeed in their ways, when they carry out their wicked schemes."
Psalm 37:7*

You have spent the school year with your class learning about waiting. Pretend you have taken a photograph of them waiting for the end of school in THE WAITING ROOM. What would your photograph look like?

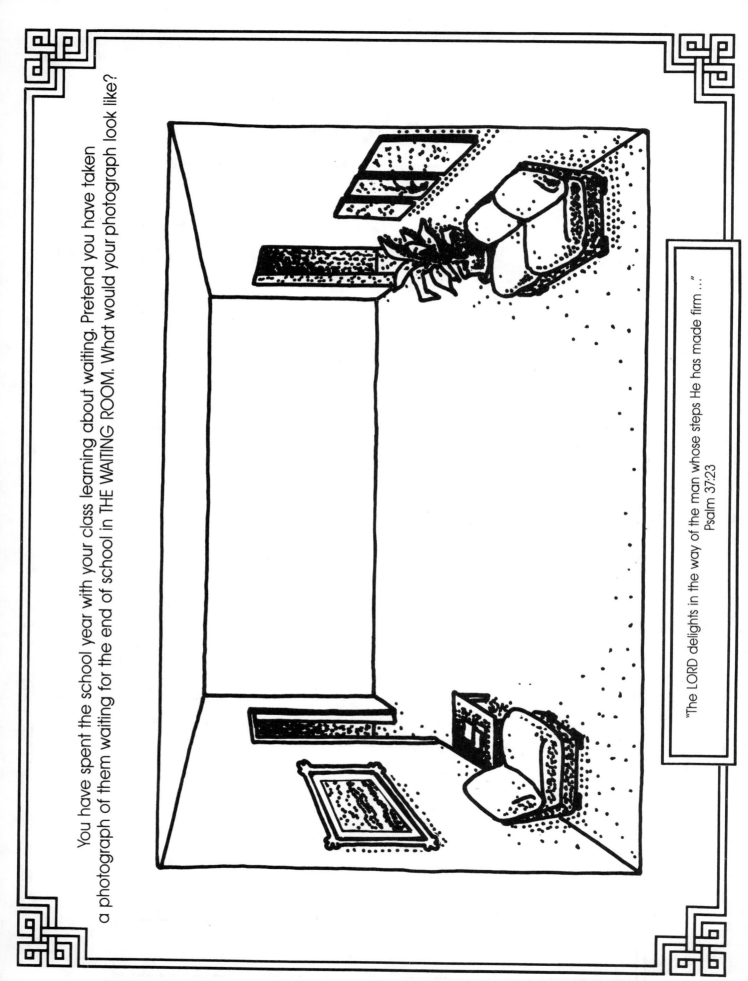

"The LORD delights in the way of the man whose steps He has made firm ..."
Psalm 37:23

Picture Yourself

Let your mind feed you pictures of yourself doing right and enjoying the life God has given you.

Picture yourself ...   **What do you see?**

Being Wise: _____

Obeying: _____

Paying Attention: _____

Trusting God: _____

Listening: _____

Showing Your Thanks: _____

Being Orderly: _____

Showing Courage: _____

Being Meek: _____

Being Loyal: _____

Feeling Joy: _____

Using Self-Control: _____

Being Honest: _____

Being Helpful: _____

Finishing a Project: _____

Having Patience: _____

Being Dependable: _____

Saying "I'm Sorry": _____

Being Fair: _____

Being Tolerant: _____

With a Good Idea: _____

Showing Love: _____

Being Resourceful: _____

Waiting: _____

"... though he stumble, he will not fall, for the LORD upholds him with his hand."
Psalm 37:24

What DON'T you have to wait for? Write your ideas here and there around this page.

**You don't have to wait for God
to start loving you.
He already does!**

NEHEMIAH

You have spent several months watching Nehemiah through words and pictures. Now you have a picture in your mind of the kind of person he was.

1. What did you like most about Nehemiah? _____
How could you be like Nehemiah in this same way? _____
_____

2. If Nehemiah and God were talking about the things they like about you, what do you think they might say? _____

3. List some things that Nehemiah had to WAIT for.
_____
_____
_____

4. If Nehemiah were able to write to you, what do you think he would tell you about:
  a. Paying attention to God's Word, the Bible?_____
  b. Obeying your parents? _____
  c. Using your good ideas to help others? _____
  d. Placing your faith in Jesus to save you a place in Heaven? _____
  e. Doing right even when some people make fun of you or scare you? _____
  f. Being willing to wait for what is best? _____

5. Think back on the things you have learned about God. Use the rest of this page to list what you like about God. It is a list He will enjoy watching you write.
_____
_____
_____
_____
_____
_____
_____

"For the LORD loves the just and will not forsake His faithful ones."
Psalm 37:28

Delight yourself in the LORD and He will give you the desires of your heart.
Commit your way to the LORD; trust in Him and He will do this:
  He will make your righteousness shine like the dawn,
    the justice of your cause like the noonday sun.
Be still before the LORD and wait patiently for Him;
    do not fret when men succeed in their ways,
    when they carry out their wicked schemes.
The LORD delights in the way of men whose steps He has made firm;
    though he stumble, he will not fall,
    for the LORD upholds him with His hand.
Turn from evil and do good;
    then you will always live securely.
For the LORD loves the just and will not forsake His faithful ones.

Psalm 37: 4-7, 23, 24, 27, 28